D1199093

CIVITAS

Scholars Press
Studies in the Humanities

Suicide

John Donne
William A. Clebsch, editor

Tragedy as a Critique of Virtue:
The Novel and Ethical Reflection

John D. Barbour

Lyric Apocalypse: Reconstruction
in Ancient and Modern Poetry

John W. Erwin

The Unusable Past: America's Puritan
Tradition, 1830 to 1930

Jan C. Dawson

The Visual Arts and Christianity
in America: The Colonial Period through
the Nineteenth Century

John Dillenberger

Chaos to Cosmos: Studies in Biblical
Patterns of Creation

Susan Niditch

Melville and the Gods

William Hamilton

The Character of the Euripidean Hippolytos:
An Ethno-Psychoanalytical Study

George Devereux

To See Ourselves As Others See Us:
Christians, Jews, "Others" in Late Antiquity

Jacob Neusner,
Ernest S. Frerichs, editors

The Riddle of Liberty:
Emerson on Alienation, Freedom, and Obedience

Lou Ann Lange

Civitas: Religious Interpetations of
the City

Peter Hawkins, editor

Scholars Press
ISBN 0-89130-987-X

CIVITAS
Religious Interpretations of the City

Edited by
Peter S. Hawkins

Scholars Press
Atlanta, Georgia

CIVITAS
Religious Interpretations of the City

Edited by
Peter S. Hawkins

©1986
Scholars Press

Library of Congress Cataloging in Publication Data

Hawkins, Peter S.
  Civitas : Christian ideas of the city.

  (Studies in the humanities)
  1. Cities and towns—History—Addresses, essays,
lectures. 2. Cities and towns—Religious aspects—
Christianity—Addresses, essays, lectures. I. Title.
II. Series: Scholars Press studies in the humanities
series.
HT111.H38 1986   307.7'6   86-1830
ISBN 0-89130-987-X

Printed in the United States of America
on acid-free paper

For Helene MacLean,
the most urbane of friends,
who has taught me much about city life
and the meaning of civility.

CONTENTS

Acknowledgments

The essays collected in this volume began as lectures delivered at Yale in the spring of 1982. The occasion was "Civitas," a symposium sponsored by the Religion and Arts Program of Yale Divinity School under the leadership of its director, Professor John W. Cook. The coherence of those initial presentations encouraged me to think of them as a potential publication. But they would not have developed into the present volume were it not for the superb editorial assistance of Ann C. Lammers, whose fine eye for detail was matched by her belief in the project as a whole. To her I am indebted not only for major help in editing, but for the collegiality that makes scholarly chores a shared enterprise to remember with pleasure. I owe a similar gratitude to Susan McShane for careful copy-editing.

Underwriting the "Civitas" symposium, and contributing toward the preparation of this volume, was a generous grant from the Henry Luce Foundation. Thanks go to its president, Mr. Robert Armstrong, as well as to Henry and Nancy Luce.

Civitas:
Religious Ideas of the City

Since the 1960s the vocabulary of urban renewal has passed quickly from the jargon of city planners and politicians into the mainstream of common speech. We speak routinely of the downtown "dying," of efforts to make the inner city "livable" again, of young gentry reclaiming an urban wilderness left desolate by shifts in urban population and affluence. This terminology first arose in an attempt to describe a complex phenomenon that followed World War II: the building of extensive highway systems leading out of town, the sprawl of suburbs, and the dead (or entirely missing) center which followed in their wake. Our commonplace talk about the city is tied, therefore, to social conditions.

Yet if we look at such language more closely—and not just between the lines, but fully at the words themselves—we find a language with mythic resonance, a vocabulary of death and resurrection. No matter how banal or unreflective the context, be it newspaper editorial or car pool conversation, talk about urban life suggests deeper levels of identification with the fate of the city than we are accustomed to acknowledge. It reveals our assumptions about the city's importance as a dimension of the imagination, as the object of immense dreams and partial fulfillments. Therefore, apart from economic and political concerns about the future, we also need to let the image of the city renew itself in our minds. For to lose it to death would be to find ourselves cut loose from moorings that are absolutely crucial to our well-being.

In his magisterial study *The City in History* (1961), Lewis Mumford identifies this inner need with the fundamentally religious aspect of urban life, that is, with its connection to the wellsprings of human identity: fear, awe, anxiety, and love. Certainly this claim is easy to demonstrate in terms of the past. Five thousand years ago, at their beginnings, cities were conceived as the dwelling-places of the gods. With its temple open to heaven, at the imagined axis of the divine and the human, the city was organized as a kind of religious theater in which eternal values might be represented and the favor of the gods secured by priest and king. The city was where heaven married earth, where earth rebelled against heaven, and where humankind experienced the mystery of its own part in the cosmic drama.

This model remained intact for millennia, *mutatis mutandis*, and until the present era. Now commercial or governmental skyscrapers play host to our civic cult, having replaced the temple as the object of visual (and cultural) attention. And yet, for all the profound changes brought about by the secularization of culture, the city continues to be the focus of ultimate concerns, the place where we manifest our values and negotiate our place in the universe. If no longer a theater in which to dramatize our relation to the divine, it remains nonetheless our central stage. It is the platform on which we simultaneously celebrate our strengths and expose our weaknesses. One has only to consider the iconography of our premier city, New York, to sense this duality of symbolic power. On the one hand it offers us the confident double assertion of the World Trade Center; on the other, the antithetical image of Charlotte Street in the South Bronx. The city stretches our limits and also reminds us of them.

Despite obvious differences that separate the essentially religious life of Mesopotamia from the increasingly secular megalopolis in which we live, the power of the city continues to galvanize our imagination, signify our aspirations, and demonstrate our mortality. And therefore, from the Uruk of *Gilgamesh* to the Oran of Camus's *La Peste*, the city remains our forum for entertaining the major questions of human existence: questions about God or God's absence; about transcendence and finitude; about the nightmares and dreams of civic life. To "read" the cities we have built or imagined is, in the end, to read the spiritual biography of our civilization.

The essays gathered here are concerned with this signifying function: what cities mean to us and what they say about us. For this reason they are not primarily interested in what classical Latin called the *urbs*, that assemblage of walls, traffic arteries, and "infrastructure" that materially constitutes an urban place. Rather, they turn our attention to the city as a symbol of human collectivity, as a "container" of corporate identity in which individuals find themselves (however imperfectly) "at home." These essays are concerned, therefore, with what classical Latin spoke of as *civitas*. Their preoccupation is with the spirit of a place rather than with the place itself; with "word cities" rather than with physical locale. They investigate the spirit that animates the body politic and that, through the media of language and art, conveys a people's notion of itself as a spiritual entity.

Civitas originally referred to the rights and privileges of the Roman *civis*, or citizen, and thus by extension to the mass of social principles that serve to organize a society and lend a specific "quality" to its life. But the term offers a far warmer, more organic sense of association than can possibly be conveyed by any definition of legal preogatives. It connotes the deepest network of cultural ties: the complex of associations, memories, and ideals that forms the spiritual matrix of life together. For the Romans, to speak of *civitas* was to point to the communal reality that coheres within a city's walls and which unites its outlying territories by a common ethos of principle and association. What it represented, therefore, was a consensus more than a constitution; it offered the city a shared lexicon of words, gestures, images and dreams. Given this extraordinary richness of meaning, with its roots deep in the unconscious and collective life of a people, it seems fitting that by the time Rome fell (and not only in the physical onslaught of the Goths, but also figuratively in the mind of the West), Latin usage should have allowed *civitas* to become a synonym for *urbs*, as if by conflating the one in the other, language was predicting the city's collapse. This is, however, a negative fantasy, and one might well say in a more optimistic mood that the merging of the two words was Latin's way of redeeming history—as if to acknowledge in the context of ruin that what truly defines a city is not its physical impregnability, but rather the values and ideals that constitute its spiritual identity. In other words, although Rome was plundered and humiliated, its *civitas* remained imperial for a millennium or more. Civic spirit long outlasted actual urban significance.

Saint Augustine is, of course, the great Christian virtuoso of *civitas*. Writing his *City of God* in response to the sack of Rome by the Visigoths in 410, he fixed his attention on the *civitas* which Rome had cultivated over the centuries and which had come to constitute its identity as divine and therefore eternal. From a detailed denunciation of its pagan values and the "false and lying gods" whose worship had introduced the seeds of destruction from the very beginning, he then turns to the vast panorama of history—a timeline which begins with the fall of the rebel angels—in which context Rome is seen as only the most recent avatar of "Babylon." It becomes the city whose god is the self, whose *civitas* is both driven and initiated by the lust for domination, whose fullest expression is hell.

What emerges from Augustine's study of history, as played out in the ongoing conflict between Satan's Babylon and God's Jerusalem, is a drama of contending notions of *civitas* to be resolved only with the Apocalypse. Drawing upon the traditional power of these biblical *topoi*, and their suggestion of states of mind and heart more than actual localities, Augustine's profoundly psychological treatment of *civitas* helped to fix in the imagination of the West a notion of the earthly city as a place of the deepest conflict and the most momentous choice—a place where "outer" and "inner," public and private, are interchangeble realities. Within the walls of any particular *urbs* at any moment in time, Augustine imagines an age-old war for the human spirit whose stakes were nothing less than citizenship for eternity, in God's city or Satan's hell.

At once betrothed by original sin to hell and wooed in grace by heaven, the city offered itself as a collective image of the human heart at war with itself. Occupying a mysteriously anomalous middle ground between the *civitas* of salvation and that of damnation, it presented itself as a "threshing floor" of tumultuous possibility and confused allegiance. As the external projection of our interior conflicts—the civic screen on which we see the dramas of the self enlarged—Augustine's notion of the earthly city is an especially vivid example of what Burton Pike has called the "reification of ambivalence." It is both damned and redeemed, a place of conflict endowed with a vision of peace. Thanks to the enormous influence of Augustine's treatise, *civitas* becomes an archetypal image of the profound contrariety within ourselves.

Augustine casts a long shadow over the essays collected in this volume, which both deals with his biblical sources and demonstrates the vitality of his Christian synthesis for subsequent works of the imagination. The chapters which comprise Part One establish a biblical and patristic background for discussion of more modern representations of *civitas* in Part Two. To begin, Robert Wilson's "The City in the Old Testament" argues against the received notion of an anti-urban bias among the ancient Hebrews. Instead, he highlights the consistently central (if ambivalent) position the city has always held in Israel's historical consciousness. From the first urban settlement founded by Cain after the loss of Eden, to the hope of an eschatological Jerusalem to fulfill the promise of King David's earthly Zion, the city is the abiding paradigm of human association, for better or worse. Personified as wife, child, murderess, and whore, it provides the collective image under which the Jews might conceive themselves in relationship with God.

Wayne Meeks shows a similar ambivalence in the writings of the New Testament, where (as in the Book of Revelation) the city is at once the great harlot, as eager for the blood of martyrs as she was for the death of Christ, and also the radiant symbol of the redeemed creation, the place where heaven and earth find their renewal, and God dwells forever with humankind. Furthermore, as he goes on to suggest in his essay, "St. Paul of the Cities," despite the country origins of the Christian faith, the authors of the New Testament writings, as well as the persons to whom they communicated, were entirely urban in their orientation. Forming themselves into self-defined and intimate communities scattered throughout the eastern Mediterranean region, the churches founded by Paul and his associates were joined together by an imperial network of cities. These early Christians knew a *civitas* of faith which set them apart from the people around them. But they also received their spiritual citizenship, and went on to share it with others, entirely within the Roman culture that claimed the whole world as its *urbs*. Looking forward (as the Epistle to the Hebrews puts it) "to the city which has foundations, whose builder and maker is God," they travelled with the news of that city over a superb system of interurban roadways maintained by the earthly city which even St. Paul could boast to the authorities was his own. Thus, with a sense of having been built up into a unified and "living temple," grafted in all their diversity into a single Body of Christ, they formed one kind of *civitas* within another—a spiritual Jerusalem within the earthly Rome.

In "Jerusalem: The City of Place," Jonathan Z. Smith focuses our attention on the unique city that preoccupies not only the Old and New

Testaments, but also the Jewish and Christian pieties that developed out of that scriptural legacy. Smith explores the relationship between city, religious hierarchy and the "technology" of ritual, to suggest how Jerusalem retained its central significance in the Judeo-Christian experience long after it ceased to have real political power. By employing a hierarchical system of status such as we find delineated in Ezekiel 40–48, with its essential distinction between pure and impure, the structure of temple and priest could be reduplicated outside (and quite apart from) the sacred place. When power failed, status endured, enabling the *civitas* of Jerusalem to travel the farthest reaches of the Diaspora.

Smith then turns from Jewish sources to the post-Constantinian Jerusalem of Eusebius and Egeria, to suggest how it was the liturgy of the Holy Sepulchre that once again made the spiritual *civitas* of Jerusalem capable of exportation to other places of Christian worship. "The structured temporality of the liturgy," he writes, "accomplished for the Christian view of Jerusalem and its church what the Jewish hierarchical structures accomplished with respect to Jerusalem and its temple." In both cases, the power of ritual placed the city at the center of a mental map that transcends the realities of actual geography.

Ambivalence toward the earthly city, and the notion of holy city/sacred place, are also important themes in Rowan A. Greer's discussion of patristic attitudes before and after the establishment of imperial Christianity. In "Alien Citizens: A Marvelous Paradox," we consider what it meant for the church to be in the world but not of it; that is, how it might keep its understanding of Christian *civitas* in dialogue with the claims of temporal community. On the one hand, there is Tertullian's rejection of the earthly Athens in favor of a heavenly Jerusalem; on the other, there are the post-Constantinian court theologians, Eusebius and Lactantius, who saw in the Christian emperor one who had brought the *civitas Dei* to earth. Between these two extremes of rejection and embrace, Greer locates the notion of "transfigured citizenship," as it was argued by Clement of Alexandria before the empire was Christianized, and by John Chrysostom afterward. What each upheld was a belief that the redeemed *civitas* could leaven the earthly lump, even as it pointed to the divine kingdom beyond the borders of space and time. Greer ends with Augustine, whose well-known polemic against the *civitas terrena* should not obscure his less-recognized conviction that earthly citizenship was of genuine importance; that Christians longing for the New Jerusalem must nonetheless "pray for the peace of Babylon." For Augustine, the post-Constantinian empire (no less than the pagan *civitas* that preceded it) is at best a place to sojourn, a "far country" in which a pilgrim must be always pressing onward. The earthly city becomes evil only when it fancies itself a residence where humans may think themselves at home. It is, Augustine says, a *temporary* good; something to be used rather than enjoyed for its own sake.

One of the options discussed in "Alien Citizens"—the more or less total identification of the earthly city with the kingdom of God—is explored by John Baldovin in "Worship in Urban Life: the Example of Medieval Constantinople." Here we see the extent to which an entire *urbs* could become the stage for celebrating a profoundly religious notion of *civitas*. Founded as an exclusively Christian city by the emperor who made his chosen faith the only legitimate religion of the empire, Constantinople could boast that its commonwealth (unlike that of Rome) had never known the worship of pagan gods. From the time of its dedication in 330 it was consecrated to Mary, Mother of God and Protector of its walls. Baldovin discusses how the city and its history were integrated into the calendar of the liturgical year, thereby keeping Constantinople alive in the worship of the Orthodox churches long after Constantinople itself became the Moslem city of Istanbul. Baldovin also suggests how the city "sanctified" itself through total urban participation in divine worship. With Hagia Sophia at its heart and streets laid out as axes of procession, liturgy became a civic event bringing together clergy, imperial court, and people. The city itself became an extended church.

In the second half of the collection, we see how these ancient issues and themes continue to nourish subsequent thinking about the city, whether in the fourteenth century or in our own time. Peter S. Hawkins's essay on Dante shows that the power of *civitas* undergirds the massive literary construction of the *Divine Comedy*, the most complex and enduring "word city" of the European Middle Ages. Arguing an Augustinian paradigm of rival civic orders to be one of the interior structures of the poem, "Nightmare and Dream: the Earthly City in Dante's *Commedia*" focuses on the peculiar position of the *civitas terrena*. Although not represented directly in this sweeping vision of the afterlife, the earthly city is nonetheless continuously evoked for us in the person of the Florentine pilgrim and through the poet's constant reference to the cities of Italy and of ancient literature alike. With Dante's own Florence at the center of attention, we see the towns of early Trecento Italy as examples of fallen creation teetering on the brink of the *civitas diaboli*. And yet, if the *Commedia* represents Florence in dour Augustinian terms as living in the shadow of hell, the poem offers another more positive image of the earthly city by way of counterbalance. For despite Dante's prophetic portrayal of the civic nightmare in which we live, he also presents the dream that lies at its heart: an earthly *civitas* patterned on the heavenly, where pope and emperor each shepherd the sheep according to their own distinctive callings, and happy urban life prepares us for the far greater joys of the heavenly Jerusalem, "that Rome where Christ is a Roman." While such a community may be nowhere in sight, it is nonetheless a birthright to be claimed by humankind—and not only in the hereafter, but in the here and now.

Dante's notion of an earthly beatitude to be realized in history and within the political sphere is still entirely grounded in the theological vision of *civitas* characteristic of the earlier Middle Ages. Its citizens remain pilgrims on their way to the City of God. Later on in the fourteenth century, however, we begin to see the development of a more secular conception of the city which in time would become the civic humanism of the Renaissance. Duncan Robinson's essay, "Fourteenth-Century Siena: the Iconography of a Medieval Commune," examines precisely this transition. Within a twenty-year frame he shows the transformation of imagery in adjacent rooms of the Sienese Palazzo Publico. Simone Martini's *Maestà* (1315) on the wall of the Council Chamber celebrates Mary as patron and queen of Siena. The painting also quite forcefully establishes the jurisdiction of the heavenly court over the public affairs of Siena. Only a generation later, however, Ambrogio Lorenzetti's allegories of Good and Bad Government (1338–1339) take us into a new and more secular era. Although the allegory of "Good Government," for instance, recalls in its iconography both sacred art and scholastic theology, the fresco is decidedly secular in its interests. It pertains not so much to the kingdom of heaven as to the mundane civic life of Siena in the Trecento, portraying as it does a realistic panorama of life and work evocative of Lorenzetti's own Tuscan landscape. Perhaps most striking of all is the dominant figure positioned close to the center of the painting: a female who is modelled not on the Virgin, but on a classical representation of Pax. Juxtaposing Lorenzetti's fresco with the Martini *Maestà*, we gain a striking contrast in notions of *civitas*. We see a vision of earthly community in which saints become civic virtues and the Queen of Heaven a personification of Siena's temporal well-being.

What Duncan Robinson helps us to realize in this contrast of one iconography and another is not so much the rejection of a religious notion of *civitas* as a relocation of attention from heaven to earth, from divine paradigm to human particularity. It is the twentieth-century outcome of this secularization that James Dougherty studies in his essay, "Exiles in the Earthly City: the Heritage of Saint Augustine." Looking back at the patristic and medieval traditions of *civitas* from the vantage point of our own mid-century, he sees in the literature of the post-World War II period an attempt to reassess and reappropriate Augustine's judgments on the earthly city. In both Auden and Camus, Dougherty finds a new appreciation for the imperfect and vulnerable in our humanity; for that *mortalitas* which Augustine condemned, but which these writers view as a common bond linking together members of the *civitas terrena*. From the rubble of bombed cities— the result of "bad government" global in its extent—there arise the ideals of rebuilding, of commitment to a common enterprise, and of compassion for one's fellows. There is a determination to construct something on which to rejoice and then build hope for the future. This reappraisal of the secular civic order is a theme noted by Dougherty also among several religious writers of the 1960s and 1970s who, though coming from a variety of theological perspectives, nevertheless see in common the earthly city as an exemplary image of our human predicament and common hope.

Although Dougherty stresses the twentieth-century revision of Augustinian thought, the writers he examines are all working within a framework of continuity rather than of rupture with the past. Thus, whatever the differences between the north Africa of Augustine and that of Camus, they share between them an archetype of the city in which associations, expectations, and ambivalences form a complex image of corporate humanity. In "The City as Cultural Hieroglyph," however, Burton Pike argues that the developments of the last hundred years have entailed such a rapid series of dislocations that the archetype of the city has been dislodged from postmodern consciousness. The city, which was a "locus of significance" from biblical times until the early twentieth century, has become something better described as a "hieroglyph": an undecipherable (and therefore, in the technical sense, insignificant) sign. To illustrate this change, Pike contrasts a late example of the archetypal city, found in a *Journal* entry of the Brothers Goncourt, with Donald Barthelme's "City Life" (1970). Pike locates Barthelme's short story in the modernist line of Eliot's *Wasteland* and Joyce's *Finnegan's Wake.* Playing off fragments of cultural memory against present-day urban anomie, Barthelme turns *civitas* into a kind of joke—an imperfect remembrance of things past which lacks cohesion, depth, or resonance. In what seems to be a new set of conventions for the city, there is no longer any center to hold to, neither a "downtown" nor any spiritual focus of urban energy. As Pike says, "Modern life is urban life; the *urbs* has finally swallowed up both the *civitas* and the *orbis.* And this *urbs* is more like a lunar landscape than a human community. There is no way to think of it as either an earthly or a heavenly Jerusalem."

This is where Pike leaves us, and where the collection comes to a close. It would seem that with Barthelme we have reached the end of a line. And yet this requiem for "city life" cannot leave us in despair, any more than it can claim to have the last word on contemporary notions of *civitas.* For at the same time at the beginning of the 1970s when Barthelme was cutting loose the city from its ancient moorings of coherence and significance, Italo Calvino in his 1972 *Imaginary Cities* was pointing to a *civitas* within the ruins, "discontinuous in space and time, now scattered, now more condensed," which may enable us to live some modicum of the just life even within "the infernal city." What Calvino describes is a secular version of Augustine's *civitas peregrina,* "a new germ of justice" that enables humanity to endure in hope. And it is precisely the apotheosis of this vision that enchants Mark Helprin's 1983 novel, *Winter's Tale,* with its quest for "the sight of a perfectly just city rejoicing in justice alone." It is this New Jerusalem of the Golden Age which the novel delivers to the reader in its closing page—a radiant and apocalyptically transformed New York of the new millennium, not unlike that city glimpsed by St. John the Divine at the end of his vision, "complex, holy, and alive." Even Barthelme himself, with the publication of a 1983 collection of stories entitled *Overnight to Many Distant Cities*, bears witness to the enduring power of an archetype that refuses to die; that continues to remind us of who we are and in what sort of universe we play our part. So deeply attached are we to the notion of *civitas*, in fact, that if cities did not exist, it would be necessary to invent them. For it is through them, finally, that we keep track of ourselves.

Part One

1

The City in the Old Testament

ROBERT R. WILSON
Yale Divinity School

I. The "Desert Ideal" in the Old Testament

> When the kingship was lowered from heaven
> the kingship was in (the city of) Eridu.
> (In) Eridu A-lulim (became) king
> and reigned 28,800 years;
> Alalgar reigned 36,000 years.
> Two kings
> reigned. . . (during) [Eridu's] 64,800 years.
> I drop (the topic of) Eridu;
> its kingship to (the city of) Bad-tibira
> was carried.[1]
>
> . . . .

Thus begins the Sumerian King List, a remarkable document in which the scribes of ancient Mesopotamia attempted for the first time to render an account of the origins of civilization as they knew it. This text, which seems to have been composed in the Mesopotamian city of Isin somewhere between 1800 and 2000 B.C.E., traces the progress of kingship from the time it was "lowered from heaven" in the city of Eridu until, after passing through a succession of cities, it came to rest in Isin. Although at first glance the King List seems to be simply a catalog of royal names, cities, and dates, in fact the text describes two of the fundamental components of the ancient Mesopotamian worldview. According to the ancient scribes, civilization itself—and therefore history itself—began only with the advent of kingship. Kingship was the gift of the gods and provided the stable hierarchical political and economic structures necessary for civilized life. Without kingship, none of the normal daily activities of Mesopotamian society could be maintained. But before there was kingship, there were cities. Their origins antedated the rise of political history, and they provided the fertile soil necessary for the

---

[1] The Sumerian King List, i. 1–10. The translation is based on the edition of Thorkild Jacobsen, *The Sumerian King List* (Chicago: University of Chicago Press, 1939), pp. 70–71.

growth of kingship. Without cities there could have been no kings. Without kings, civilization itself could not have developed.[2]

When we look back at the extraordinary importance that the Mesopotamian scribes attached to cities, we are struck by the differences between this view of cities and the one we often associate with the early Hebrews. We tend to think of Israel's ancestors as wanderers and nomads, people who were uncomfortable in cities and who deplored the cultural and theological evils they associated with them. This notion that Israel had a negative opinion of cities is not confined to casual readers of the Bible. It has also been held by a number of biblical scholars. According to the standard scholarly view, the early Hebrews were nomads who eventually drifted out of the desert and into the settled land of Canaan but never gave up the ideals of their early nomadic existence. They considered the Canaanite cities politically and socially corrupt and feared the harmful effects of urban religious practices on Israel's faithfulness to the desert God, Yahweh. Scholars who hold this view tend to interpret all Israelite religious history against the background of Israel's supposed antiurban views and its faithfulness to the religion of its nomadic past. Thus the prophets are to be seen as preservers of Israel's nomadic traditions and constant critics of religion and life in the Canaanite cities.

For some prophets, according to this argument, Israel's chief sin was its rejection of nomadic religion and its adulterous love affair with the fertility cults maintained in the cities. Thus, for example, Jeremiah seems to look back nostalgically at the period of Israel's wanderings in the wilderness and to see it as a time when Israel was absolutely faithful to Yahweh its God: "I remember the devotion of your youth, your love as a bride; how you followed me in the wilderness in a land not sown" (Jer. 2.2). Similarly, Hosea deplores the corruption of the cities and prophesies the coming of a day when Yahweh will remove the people of Israel from the cities and take them back to the wilderness, where the pure worship of God can be reinstated:

> Therefore, behold, I will allure her, and bring her into the wilderness, and speak tenderly to her. And there she shall answer as in the days of her youth, as at the time when she came out of the land of Egypt. . . . I will remove the names of the Baals from her mouth, and they shall be mentioned by name no more. . . . And I will betroth you to me forever; I will betroth you to me with righteousness and with justice, with

---

[2] For a discussion of the origins and functions of the Sumerian King List and its view of cities, see Giorgio Buccellati, "The Enthronement of the King and the Capital City in Texts from Ancient Mesopotamia and Syria," in *Studies Presented to A. Leo Oppenheim* (Chicago: Oriental Institute of the University of Chicago, 1964), pp. 54–61; William W. Hallo, "The Beginning and End of the Sumerian King List in the Nippur Recension," *Journal of Cuneiform Studies* 17 (1963): 52–57; Robert R. Wilson, *Genealogy and History in the Biblical World* (New Haven: Yale University Press, 1977), pp. 73–83; and William W. Hallo, "Antediluvian Cities," *Journal of Cuneiform Studies* 23 (1970): 57–67.

> steadfast love and with mercy. I will betroth you to me with faithfulness;
> and you shall know the Lord. (Hos. 2.14–20)

Thus, at the end of days the prophet hopes for a return to Israel's nomadic origins.[3]

The major difficulty with this view that Israel had an antiurban bias is that it cannot be found in the Old Testament text. The only two passages that seem to glorify the wilderness ideal and to imply a negative opinion of cities are the ones from Jeremiah and Hosea that I have just quoted. However, in both cases an antiurban reading can be obtained only by ignoring the contexts in which the wilderness references are set. Thus, scholars who want to see in Jeremiah a rejection of city life usually stress the one verse which looks nostalgically at the period of Israel's wilderness wanderings, but they minimize the importance of the whole oracle which immediately follows the verse:

> Thus says the Lord: "What wrong did your ancestors find in me that they went far from me and went after worthlessness and became worthless? They did not say, 'Where is the Lord who brought us up from the land of Egypt, who led us in the wilderness, in a land of deserts and pits, in a land of drought and deep darkness, in a land that none passes through, where no one dwells?' And I brought you into a plentiful land to enjoy its fruits and its good things. But when you came in you defiled my land, and made my heritage an abomination." (Jer. 2.5–7)

This hardly sounds like the exaltation of life in the desert at the expense of life in the Canaanite cities. The wilderness is described as a hostile place, which resembles nothing so much as the underworld itself, the realm of the dead, the very antithesis of life. Like the underworld, the wilderness is described as a land of dangerous traps for the unwary, a land of drought and supernatural darkness where no light penetrates, a land of no return, where no one lives.[4] The point of the oracle is that Yahweh led Israel *through* this

---

[3] For discussions of the "nomadic ideal" in ancient Israel, see Karl Budde, "The Nomadic Ideal in the Old Testament," *The New World* 4 (1895): 726–45; John W. Flight, "The Nomadic Idea and Ideal in the Old Testament," *Journal of Biblical Literature* 42 (1923): 158–226; Samuel Nystrom, *Beduinentum and Jahwismus* (Lund: C. W. K. Gleerup, 1946); and the recent popular work of Morris S. Seale, *The Desert Bible* (New York: Saint Martin's, 1974). For more balanced treatment of the issue, see Niels-Erik Andreasen, "Town and Country in the Old Testament," *Encounter* 42 (1981): 259–75; James Muilenburg, "Biblical Images of the City," in Robert Lee, ed., *The Church and the Exploding Metropolis* (Richmond: John Knox Press, 1965), pp 45–59; Giorgio Buccellati, *Cities and Nations of Ancient Syria* (Rome: Istituto di studi del vicino oriente, 1967); and Frank S. Frick, *The City in Ancient Israel* (Missoula: Scholars Press, 1977).

[4] Compare the description of the underworld found at the beginning of the Akkadian myth of the Descent of Ishtar to the Nether World (obverse, ll.1–11). The text is published as *CT* 15.45–48 and translated in James B. Pritchard, ed., *Ancient Near Eastern Texts Relating to the Old Testament* (Princeton: Princeton University Press, 1969), pp. 106–9.

dreadful land and into the life-giving land of Canaan, a land which, Deuteronomy tells us, was already filled with orchards, vineyards, cisterns, houses, and, of course, cities (cf. Deut. 6.10–11). Jeremiah fondly remembers the wilderness *period* but not the wilderness itself. He remembers that Israel faithfully followed Yahweh in the wilderness, as Yahweh led them out of the wilderness and into the inhabited land.

In the same way, Hosea's eschatological return to the wilderness does not glorify the wilderness itself but speaks of restoring a trusting and faithful marital relationship between Yahweh and Israel. The reason for the return to the wilderness becomes apparent in the verses immediately following the last one quoted from Hosea: "And in that day, says the Lord, I will answer the heavens and they shall answer the earth; and the earth shall answer the grain, the wine and the oil, and they shall answer Jezreel; and I will sow her [i.e., Israel] for myself in the land" (Hos. 2.21–23). The goal of the preparation in the wilderness is a new exodus from the wilderness and a new entry into the land, a land characterized by its fruitfulness and by its cities.

If these passages cannot be used to support the notion that biblical Israel harbored a latent hostility toward cities, then what do the Old Testament texts tell us about Israel's views of the city? The best place to begin a reconstruction of Israelite attitudes toward cities is in the accounts of the people's early history.

II. Cities in Israelite Myth and History

In contrast to the commonly held opinion that the Israelites were relative latecomers to cities, Israel's own accounts of its origins places the creation of cities at the very beginning of human life on earth. Cain, after killing his brother Abel, is said to have fled to a foreign land, where either he or his son Enoch built the first city. The city then became the matrix for the development of other aspects of civilization. Cain's descendants became the first tent dwellers and cattle keepers, but they also became the first to develop those special skills usually associated with the city. They became the first artists and musicians, and they were the first artisans to create implements of bronze and iron (Gen. 4.17–22). According to the Israelite historian, the first place where humans dwelled permanently was not the Garden of Eden or the field where Cain killed his brother, but the city. It was in the city that life as the historian knew it—as we know it—began to grow.

It is important to notice, though, that the Israelite writers did not confuse the garden and the city. The Garden of Eden was considered an ideal place, where God's carefully created order was supposed to be maintained by the first humans, who were to live in harmony with the whole creation, with each other, and with God. But the people could not live in the garden. They upset God's orderly creation and ultimately fled to the one place where they could live: the city. Like the garden, the city was a creative place, a place which gave birth to the arts and sciences. Yet, unlike the garden, the city also had characteristics that could be destructive and even demonic. The city was not one large harmonious family. It was an uneasy amalgam of individuals who were sometimes hostile toward each other. It was a place of refuge for criminals and for people who had left their families or been driven out to sustain themselves as best they could. It was a place of anonymity and isolation, which could sometimes lead to violence. Cain's descendant Lamech was not only the father of the first artists and artisans, but also the creator of the first war song celebrating vengeance over his enemies (Gen. 4.23–24).

The Israelite historian's notion that the city was both creative and destructive is further developed in the famous story of the tower of Babel. On the one hand, the city and its tower are depicted as monuments to human creativity, organization, and skill. In the middle of an unproductive and potentially dangerous plain, the builders make for themselves a refuge, using all the technological skills traditionally associated with cities. Overcoming the lack of raw materials in their environment, they create their own building materials, using brick instead of stone and pitch instead of mortar. They then work together to construct a city and a gigantic tower, a tower so tall and architecturally complex that its top will touch the heavens themselves. In the eyes of the builders, this monument to human achievement will protect them from outside attack and prevent them from being scattered over the earth. The city and its defensive tower will provide the builders with a kind of artificial unity. The city's walls will enclose its heterogeneous inhabitants, molding them into a single group and even providing access to the heavens. The city is rightly called Babel (in Akkadian *bāb ili*), which means "the gate of God," for it is the locus of communication between the human and divine worlds; but it is primarily a testimony to human, not divine achievement, to the ability of disparate people to organize themselves and create together something for the common good. The city builders even believe that their creative skills can overcome the transitoriness of their lives. The city will make for them a name which will survive after they themselves have departed.

But the Israelite historian realizes that this ideal view of the city cannot match the reality. The writer therefore describes how God alters the grandiose plans of the builders, in the process underscoring all the city's imperfections. Because of God's intervention the city is never completed. Heterogeneity is not overcome but actually intensified when God confuses the language of the builders. *Bāb-ēl*, The Gate of God, is associated by the writer with the Hebrew word *bālal*, "to confuse." The city never realizes its builders' dreams. It was to serve as a place of refuge, but in the end it cannot protect its inhabitants from being scattered throughout the earth. Thus, if the city is the preeminent example of human organization and creativity, it is also an uneasy association of hostile individuals who cannot communicate with each other, and who will ultimately go their own ways. The city therefore embodies not only the potential for a harmonious life but also the divisive tensions which tend to destroy civilization.

It is important to notice that the Israelite historian places no explicit value on either the creative or the destructive forces within the city. Rather, by telling this mythical story of the city of Babel, the writer paints a rather sophisticated picture of real cities that Israel knew from its experience. Israel recognized that it had to make its peace with the city, maximizing the creative potential while minimizing the problems of urban life.

It is with this complex understanding of the nature of cities that the biblical historian begins the narrative of Israel's ancestors. As the story unfolds, from the call of Abraham until the final occupation of Canaan, the people of Israel will always be associated with cities. Israel's ancestor, Abraham, is remembered as a city dweller, living in the cities of Ur and Haran, until he left his family to travel to a new land at God's direction. The texts describe Abraham and his immediate descendants as wanderers, who had no permanent dwelling but lived temporarily in or near various cities. The ancestors met some of their immediate needs by farming or by keeping flocks of sheep and goats, but they depended on nearby cities to supply other goods and services. Some of the ancestors are actually said to have founded cities, while others are pictured as settling in cities and becoming part of their political structure. Indeed, the urban activities of one of these ancestors, Joseph, are said to have led to Israel's captivity in Egypt and subsequent liberation by Yahweh.

After a period of wandering and purification in the wilderness, Yahweh finally fulfilled the promise to Abraham by bringing the people to the land of Canaan. The conquest narratives report that after suitable warnings about the dangers and temptations in the cities of the inhabited land, the people of Israel invade the land, capturing the cities they were able to overcome and slowly infiltrating others. From that point on the Israelites became permanent city dwellers, and Israel's national and religious life was bound up with the fate of its cities.

The general outlines of this biblical picture agree tolerably well with recent archaeological and ethnographic reconstructions of Israel's origins. The evidence suggests that the Hebrews first appeared on the stage of history as part of the widespread migration of tribal groups that covered most of Mesopotamia during the second millennium B.C.E. Some of these groups seem to have been unified by kinship ties, while others were composed of stateless individuals who had been driven out of their tribes or had left voluntarily because the tribal economy was unable to support them. These small groups of individuals seem to have gravitated to the cities, living either on the fringes of settled areas or within the cities themselves. Some groups carried out farming and herding activities outside the cities and supplied the produce, wool, and meat upon which urban dwellers depended but which they could not produce themselves. In return, the cities supplied the herders and agriculturalists with specialized services and manufactured goods. However, individuals from other groups apparently took advantage of the anonymity of the cities and settled in them permanently. In the cities family ties and personal histories were unimportant, and individuals with marketable skills could easily be absorbed into urban populations. This process of slow infiltration was presumably to work not only in the period of the ancestors but also in the period of the conquest, when in some cities settled Israelites may have joined with dissatisfied elements of the native population to overthrow their Canaanite rulers. In any case, by the end of the conquest period Israel was firmly in control of many of the Canaanite cities, a process which was finally completed by the military activities of David.[5]

However, David was not only responsible for extending Israelite control to all of the cities within his borders. He also made a brilliant and decisive move that forever altered Israelite views of the city. After capturing the old Jebusite city of Jerusalem, he made it his political capital. Because the city was not in the territory of any of the tribes, it was considered David's personal possession and was forever after called "the city of David." The king then moved the old ark of the covenant into the city, established a priesthood, and made his own capital city the religious center of Israel. The city of David thus also became the city of God.[6]

From these roots grew one of the most powerful theological concepts in ancient Israelite religion, the so-called royal Zion theology.[7] According to Jerusalem's royal theologians, Yahweh had promised David an eternal royal line in Jerusalem. One of his descendants would always sit upon Israel's throne. At the same time, Yahweh had elected Jerusalem as the divine dwelling place forever. Yahweh promised to remain eternally in the city. Israel's political and religious lives were firmly linked together, and both were inextricably bound to a single city, the city of Jerusalem. The fully developed Zion theology has marked many Old Testament passages, but it is most clearly visible in the so-called Zion psalms, such as psalm 132:

> The Lord swore to David a sure oath
> from which he will not turn back:
> One of the sons of your body
> I will set on your throne.
> If your sons keep my covenant
> and my testimonies which I shall teach them,

[5] For a survey of recent theories on Israel's conquest of Canaan and the rise of the monarchy, see John H. Hayes and J. Maxwell Miller, eds., *Israelite and Judaean History* (Philadelphia: Westminster Press, 1977), pp. 213–363.

[6] For a discussion of the importance of this event, see Martin Noth, "Jerusalem and the Israelite Tradition," in his *The Laws in the Pentateuch and Other Studies* (Philadelphia: Fortress Press, 1967), pp. 132–44.

[7] For a discussion of the royal Zion theology, see Ronald E. Clements, *God and Temple* (Oxford: Basil Blackwell, 1965), pp. 40–78.

> their sons also forever
> shall sit upon your throne.
> For the Lord has chosen Zion;
> he has desired it for his habitation:
> "This is my resting place forever;
> here I will dwell, for I have desired it."
> (Ps. 132.11–14)

Politics and religion are now firmly tied together, and from a theological perspective, Israel's concern for cities has been reduced to concern for a single city. The fate of Jerusalem is now the fate of the whole of Israelite civilization.

III. The Eschatological City

Israel's belief in the eternal election of Jerusalem was severely tested when the Babylonians besieged the city in 587 B.C.E. and deported the king, together with many of his officials. Nevertheless, because the Babylonian king installed a Davidic ruler on the throne, it was still possible for Jerusalemites to claim that God had not broken the promise to David but had simply punished the city for its sins. Even when an ill-advised revolt against Babylon again brought an enemy army to the gates of the city, prophets rooted in the royal theology could still promise that Jerusalem would never fall and that the Davidic king would remain on the throne (Jer. 23.17). Then in 587 B.C.E. the Babylonians breached the walls, deported the king and most of the remaining officials, sacked the city, and burned the temple. The Davidic dynasty came to an end, and the possibility of its restoration seemed remote. In the opinion of some of the exiles, God had actually deserted the temple and turned the city over to the Babylonians (Ezek. 9.1–11.25). The era of Jerusalem's election seemed to be at an end.

Yet even in the dark days of the exile, hope for the restoration of the city remained. Unnamed prophets in this period still spoke of Israel's triumphant return to Zion and looked forward to the day when God would again dwell in Jerusalem (Isa. 2.2–4). The prophet Ezekiel and his followers even sketched elaborate building plans for the rebuilding of the temple and the city (Ezek. 40–48).

Nowhere is Israel's hope more strongly expressed than in the writings of the anonymous prophet of the exile whom we call Deutero-Isaiah. When the Persians overran the Babylonian empire, the prophet saw in these events the working out of God's plan to return the exiles to Zion (Isa. 44.26–28). The city which had seemed forsaken would again be remembered by God, and with the return of the exiles Jerusalem would resume its position as an exalted city, one which resembled the fabled garden of Eden:

> For the Lord will comfort Zion;
> he will comfort all her waste places,

and will make her wilderness like Eden,
her desert like the garden of the Lord;
joy and gladness will be found in her,
thanksgiving and the voice of song.
. . . .
And the ransomed of the Lord shall return,
and come to Zion with singing;
everlasting joy shall be upon their heads;
they shall obtain joy and gladness,
and sorrow and sighing shall flee away.
(Isa. 51.3, 11; cf. 49.14–23)

Jerusalem would be transformed into a holy city which would fulfill its original destiny as the dwelling place of Yahweh and the center of religious truth. Thus, Deutero-Isaiah calls to the city:

Awake, awake,
put on your strength, O Zion;
put on your beautiful garments,
O Jerusalem, the holy city;
for there shall no more come into you
the uncircumcised and the unclean.
. . . .
Hark, your watchmen lift up their voice;
together they sing for joy;
for eye to eye they see
the return of the Lord to Zion (Isa. 52.1, 8).

In Deutero-Isaiah's vision of a restored Jerusalem, the city would not only resume its place as Israel's religious capital but would actually play a direct role in spreading the good news of God's return. As a symbol of the whole nation of Israel, Jerusalem would become God's servant to establish justice in the land and to teach all of the nations God's law. As the exiles returned to Zion, the city itself would give forth to the rest of the cities of Judah the joyful report that God had once again taken up residence in Jerusalem:

Get you up to a high mountain,
O Zion, herald of good tidings;
lift up your voice with strength,
O Jerusalem, herald of good tidings;
lift up; fear not;
say to the cities of Judah,
"Behold your God." (Isa. 40.9)

While Deutero-Isaiah's words helped to give hope to exilic Israel and inspired the people to return to Jerusalem, the prophet also caused them to have unrealistic expectations about the nature of the return. The restored Jerusalem was not the expected garden of Eden but a very human city, where warring factions argued among themselves about the rules which

would govern political and religious life. Even the long-awaited rebuilding of
the temple did not lead to religious harmony, and there were acrimonious
disputes about the practical aspects of temple construction (Ezra 3.1–13).
Furthermore, the political situation did not improve. The Davidic monarchy
was not restored, and the actual control of the government remained in the
hands of a succession of foreign powers. Those who had been influenced by
the hopeful oracles of Deutero-Isaiah began to feel as if the exile had not
really ended at all, even though Jerusalem was once again inhabited.

In response to these new feelings of frustration about conditions in
Jerusalem, prophets again began to deliver oracles promising a solution to
Jerusalem's problems and a final vindication of God's eternal promise to the
city. However, instead of learning from earlier Israelite writers, who had
realistic views of the city as a place where creativity and destruction, harmony and discord uneasily coexist, these late prophetic writers tended to
amplify the same idealistic themes that had been used by Deutero-Isaiah. As
a result, Israel's view of cities in general and the city of Jerusalem in
particular began increasingly to diverge from reality. Zion would be exalted,
and the enemies of Israel would be punished, even though a major transformation of reality might be required to accomplish these ends:

> For behold, I create new heavens and a new earth;
> and the former things shall not be remembered
> or come into mind.
> But be glad and rejoice forever in that which I create;
> for behold, I create Jerusalem a rejoicing,
> and her people a joy.
> I will rejoice in Jerusalem, and be glad in my people;
> no more shall be heard in it the sound of weeping
> and the cry of distress.
> . . . .
> The wolf and the lamb shall feed together,
> the lion shall eat straw like the ox;
> and dust shall be the serpent's food.
> they shall not hurt or destroy in all my holy mountain.
> (Isa. 65.17–19, 25)

Just as there was an increasing tendency to portray Jerusalem as the
Garden of Eden, a place where Israel's early ancestors realized they were not
at home, so too there was an increasing tendency to stress the role of
Jerusalem as a holy city. It was to be a city set apart, where the unclean and
the unrighteous could not enter:

> And on that day there shall be inscribed on the bells
> of the horses, "holy to the Lord"; and the pots in the
> house of the Lord shall be as bowls before the
> altar; and every pot in Jerusalem shall be sacred to
> the Lord of Hosts. . . . (Zech. 14.20–21)

Thus, God's promise to dwell in Jerusalem will be fulfilled at the end of time. Jerusalem remains the eternal dwelling place of God. But in the process Jerusalem has been transformed into something that is no longer recognizable as a human city. The original vision of the Israelite historian has been lost. The city is no longer a mixture of good and evil, but in the final vision of Jerusalem in the Old Testament, the city is a divine city where no normal human being can live. The task of reclaiming the city's human dimensions was left to future generations of Jews and Christians, who would have to solve for themselves the problem of relating the divine in the city to the human.

2
Saint Paul of the Cities

WAYNE A. MEEKS
Yale University

The elite troops of the praetorian guard in the high Roman Empire used to sneer at civilians by calling them *pagani*—"country folk," "people from the boondocks," Jean Gagé, the social historian who calls attention to this slang, points out that it is rooted in the deep prejudice that urban and rural people had against each other in antiquity.[1] A few centuries later, the Christian *militia christi*, confident in their new triumphalism, would apply the same tag to their opponents, the adherents of the old religions: "pagans."

In the New Testament itself there is a certain ambivalence about the city, but there can be little doubt that the books were written by people whose perspective was urban.[2] True, the Revelation of John portrays *the* city, the *urbs romana*, as "a great harlot," astride a monster with seven heads, drunk with the blood of the martyrs. At her downfall the faithful multitude watch from heaven as the flames consume her, and they sing, "Hallelujah! The smoke from her goes up for ever and ever." Nevertheless, what they are looking forward to is another city, the New Jerusalem, that comes down from heaven to earth. At the last day the church comes in from the wilderness and dwells in a pure and marvelous city forever. Like the ancient models of faith catalogued in the Epistle to the Hebrews, they are tired of camping in tents; they look forward "to the city which has foundations, whose builder and maker is God."

Early Christianity was an urban movement. That is well known, but we forget how important this fact was for its whole development. Sunday school images of Bedouin robes, of peasants and shepherds and the Galilean fishermen of Jesus' parables, are so deep-rooted in our minds. Yet if Christianity had remained a village movement, we would probably never have heard of it.

---

[1] Jean Gagé, *Les Classes sociales dans l'empire romain* (Paris: Payot, 1964), p.135.
[2] This essay has beed adapted from my book *The First Urban Christians: The Social World of the Apostle Paul* (New Haven and London: Yale University Press, 1983), particularly chapter 1.

It was in the cities that it discovered the means to spread across the empire in a time so short that we still find it astonishing. It was the city that shaped its language, its institutions, even its beliefs.

Among the urban forms of early Christianity, there is one about which we know a great deal: the congregations founded by Paul and his associates. Paul's world was a world of cities. When he wants to say, "I've been in trouble in every possible place," he lists "danger in the city, danger in the wilderness, danger at sea" (2 Cor. 11.26). What is missing is the productive countryside, the *chōra*, on which the whole economy of ancient society depended. For Paul, outside the city there is just nothing—*erēmia*. He belonged to those circles who depended for their livelihood entirely on the city. Urban perspective seems to have been typical of those who joined the groups he founded. This fact helps us to understand how Paul could brag to the Roman Christians, "I have fulfilled the gospel from Jerusalem round to Illyricum." Practically, what did he mean? He had left behind a handful of believers in each of a dozen or so scattered cities, each group meeting in someone's dining room. Yet, in his view of things, those few strategically located cities filled the Eastern world.

Paul served his apprenticeship as a Christian missionary in Antioch-on-the-Orontes. Antioch was one of the three or four most important cities of the empire. It was the center of political, military, and commercial traffic between Rome and the Persian frontier, and between Palestine and Asia Minor. There was in Antioch a large and vigorous Jewish community. In that setting Paul's predecessors and coworkers developed the form of missionary practice that we know best from his letters. This form of missionary activity was probably characteristic of most of the urban expansion of the movement.

After the confrontation with Peter in Antioch, Paul seems to have detached himself from the church there and formed a new circle of his own. A remarkable network now grew up of traveling apostles, local leaders, and emissaries—"coworkers," as Paul called them. The center of their activity moved westward into Asia Minor, Macedonia, and mainland Greece. If we limit ourselves to the evidence from the letters of Paul and his immediate disciples, we find that the Pauline movement took root in at least four provinces of the Roman Empire: Galatia, Asia, Macedonia, and Achaia. The cities where there were Pauline churches ranged from little towns like Philippi and the rustic but proud centers of the Celtic tribal kingdoms in Galatia, to sprawling metropolises like Ephesus and Corinth. At least two were Roman colonies: Philippi and Corinth, quite different from each other. Philippi was mainly an agricultural center, Corinth a center of crafts and commerce. Yet all were, in their institutions, their public face, and the pride of their citizens, cities. Except for the two Latin colonies, their common language was Greek—and even in Corinth and Philippi Greek was the natural language of many, perhaps most, of the population. All except Philippi were trading centers, and even there a good many foreign residents earned their living by trade. All were well located for easy access by sea, by land, or both. All were connected by good Roman roads.

The cities of the Mediterranean world were at the leading edge of the great political and social changes that occurred during the six-and-a-half centuries from Alexander to Constantine. It was Alexander who made the city the vehicle of a new cultural vision. "Urbanization" became the means of "hellenization." His successors and then the Romans made the chartering of cities the means of empire-building and exploitation. Since Rostovtseff it has been customary to speak of "urbanization" as the conscious policy of the emperors from Augustus to Hadrian. The word may be misleading. What happened was not the building of many new cities. Rather, Roman or Greek types of charters were granted to existing urban clusters. The point of the policy was to build a network of interdependence, primarily between the Roman aristocracy, old or new, and the aristocracy of the provincial cities. Glen Bowersock, for example, has shown how adroitly Augustus used patronage to make the upper classes of the Eastern cities dependent on himself.[3] In exchange for their loyalty and the support of their own clienteles, he gave them protection and forwarded their own careers and those of their sons.

Rome thus did two things for the cities of the Greek East. First, from the time of Octavian's victory over Antony, it gave them an era of unprecedented stability and opportunity to prosper. That relatively happy age lasted for a century. Second, as a consequence of Rome's entry into the East and her active interest in the cities, urban society became somewhat more complex than it had been even during the Hellenistic age. The power of Rome, superimposed on the old order, skewed the relationships of power and produced certain kinds of movement.

The simplest and most obvious kind of movement was physical. We all know about the Roman roads, and their fame is fully deserved. The imperial government now took responsibility for building and maintaining those roads. Moreover, Roman military presence kept down brigandage on land routes and virtually cleared the Mediterranean of pirates. People still complained routinely about the dangers and discomforts of travel, but nevertheless they traveled. The roads were thick with people journeying for all sorts of reasons. There were the armies and the civil service—at both the consular and the equestrian levels—and the bureaucracy of Caesar's household. There were merchants on their way to suppliers or to market; young men of rank going away for a university education; slaves on business for their masters; sick people and hypochondriacs, like Aelius Aristides in the second century, going to Epidaurus or Pergamum to take a cure; sightseers and religious pilgrims; and so on.

[3] Glen W. Bowersock, *Augustus and the Greek World* (Oxford: Clarendon, 1965), pp. 29–41.

Not only was this the age of travel; it was also the age of long-term migrations: veterans who were settled in new colonies by the emperor; merchants and artisans looking for better markets; persons enslaved and displaced by war or piracy and later freed; political exiles; soldiers of fortune. Immigration was the most common way in which religions moved and changed. Very often these noncitizen residents *(metoikoi)* gathered with others from the same homeland and formed an association to retain their identity and, when need or opportunity arose, to use their corporate power to negotiate for privileges in the city. Thus on the island of Delos one is still impressed by the monuments erected beside the harbor facilities by the Italian merchants, and by the elegant clubhouse erected near the famous Lion Terrace by the "Association of the Poseidoniasts of Berytus." On a smaller scale, the temples of the Egyptian and Syrian gods on the acropolis above Philippi attest the strength and organization of the corresponding immigrant communities there. One of the terms occasionally used for such a community organization was the *synagōgē*, the "gathering," of such-and-such. Of course, the Jews were a special case of this phenomenon—special because their loyalty to one God barred them from participating in any other cult, even in the routine cults of the city itself. This loyalty made them seem aloof and strange to those accustomed to the genial tolerance and pluralism of hellenistic and Roman religious sentiment. Nevertheless, their presence in the cities and the centering of their communal life in the cult of their ancestral deity were understandable and familiar.

It is more problematic to speak of social mobility in the Roman Empire, and more difficult to assess its importance for religious change. The rule of thumb is that there was *no* social mobility to speak of. People stayed put in the social pyramid. As the late Cambridge historian A. H. M. Jones put it, "On the whole the classes were hereditary. The rich landowning families served generation after generation on the city councils. Sons of soldiers followed their fathers in the legions and the *auxilia*. Peasant proprietors cultivated their ancestral holdings, and tenants likewise."[4] Nevertheless, there were exceptions. Barbara Levick, for example, has traced the careers of two veterans in the colony of Antioch-in-Pisidia. They were of obscure, lower-class Italian origin; their family names were and are literally unknown. Yet in Augustus's new colony they found room for their talents. Wealth and power followed. Their descendants would not only sit on the municipal council of the colony, but be enrolled in the Roman Senate.[5]

Among the few people who were able to rise above their parents' social level, apart from the rich who regularly got richer, freedmen "stood out," as

---

[4] Arnold H. M. Jones, "The Caste System in the Later Roman Empire," *Eirene* 8 (1970): 89.

[5] Barbara M. Levick, *Roman Colonies in Southern Asia Minor* (Oxford: Clarendon, 1967), pp. 103–20.

Ramsay MacMullen has observed.[6] This was especially the case in Rome, but in certain circumstances also in the East. Strabo tells us that when Julius Caesar refounded Corinth, he colonized it "with people that belonged for the most part to the freedmen class."[7] With no indigenous aristocracy to snub them or to frustrate their ambitions, the freedmen colonists had the rare opportunity to compete with one another for the marks of status that would enable some of them to *become* the local aristocracy. They did so in the ways well known in the Greco-Roman cities: they gave conspicuous presents to the city in return for offices and public honors. One of the loveliest monuments that has been reconstructed in the upper forum of Corinth was a little temple erected in the reign of Tiberius by Cornelius Babbius Philinus. He had been a freedman, of Greek origin. An inscription emblazoned on the monument tells us that he served as *aedile* and then, "in return for his generous gifts, the colony made him *pontifex* and *duumvir.*" Similar, though less prominent, was a certain Erastus, who a couple of decades later paved the square east of the theater's stage building "in return for his aedileship, at his own expense." Perhaps he was the same Erastus who shortly before had been "treasurer of the city" and a member of the Christian community at Corinth (Rom. 16.23). Such cases of upward social mobility were rare. The point is that when they did happen, they happened in cities. Many people traveled to cities, then as now, in quest of a better life. Occasionally (more seldom then than now) they found it.

The cities were the places where power was exercised. They were the places where the empire took shape. They were places where coalitions could be built. Jews, for example, learned how to play off imperial power against the power of local aristocracies. The Roman emperor and his governors were playing a similar game.

The cities were places where changes could occur. The central characteristic of villages, MacMullen points out, was their conservatism.[8] People living at the edge of subsistence do not often take risks. If some extraordinary circumstance impelled a villager to seek change—a lucky inheritance, a religious vision, money saved up—it was to the city that he went.

The changes that occurred in the city were in the direction of a common Greco-Roman culture. The conservatism of the villages preserved their diversity. The simplest instance is language. Even today one can travel through Turkey and Greece in reasonable comfort, using only English or German, so long as one stays in the cities. Once in the villages, however, even knowing the national language one may still have difficulty with local dialects or pronunciations. The contrast in antiquity was much sharper.

[6] Ramsay MacMullen, *Roman Social Relations 50 B.C. to A.D. 284* (New Haven and London: Yale University Press, 1974), p. 100.

[7] Strabo, *Geog.* 8.6.23, C381.

[8] MacMullen, p. 27.

Greek was the language of the cities, but beginning only a few miles beyond their walls the old native languages held sway. It is no accident that every document in the New Testament and most other extant Christian literature from the first two centuries was composed in Greek. It was mainly in the cities that the early Christians found their distinctive voice.

Let us return to those urban missionaries about whom we know most, Paul and his comrades. When Paul, Silas, Timothy, Titus, and the others arrived in a city to preach the gospel, where and how did they begin? How did they make connection with those who would listen? The book of Acts portrays the missionaries always beginning in the synagogues. We cannot accept this picture at face value, however, for Paul describes his mission as directed to the gentiles from the beginning. On the other hand, Acts cannot be entirely wrong, for Paul reports that he was flogged by Jewish authorities five times (2 Cor. 11.24). If he never went near the synagogues, those punishments would be hard to explain. Thus the little vignette about the first mission in Philippi (Acts 16) seems true to life. On the Sabbath the missionaries went "outside the gate to the riverside, where we supposed there was a place of prayer" (Acts 16.13). There they met Lydia, a gentile worshipper of the Jewish God, an alien merchant in Philippi. Later the same author tells us that in Corinth Paul "found a Jew named Aquila," who with his wife, Prisca, ran a tent-making shop.

We have to assume, then, that when a stranger arrived in a city, he knew or could easily learn where to find immigrants and temporary residents from his own country or people, and practitioners of his own trade. Nothing could be more natural; that was the way neighborhoods were organized in most ancient cities.The Jewish quarter would be easily discoverable. The Linen-weavers' Quarter, the Leatherworkers' Street, the Portico of the Perfumers would be identified by signs carved at street corners. Christian travelers began by finding people like themselves.

Below the level of the ethnic quarter and neighborhood came the individual household. This was the basic unit of Christianity in the city; it was the basic unit of society itself. Acts and the letters agree on the importance of the conversion of whole households and depict the house as the meeting place of the Christian cell. We have to bear in mind that when the New Testament speaks of Stephanas and his household, or Lydia and hers, the word "household" refers to a more extended conglomerate of relationships than our modern nuclear family. "Family" was not defined primarily by kinship but by the relationship of dependence and subordination on the one hand, and protection on the other. The head of a substantial house was responsible for—and expected a degree of obedience from—not only his immediate family but also his slaves, his former slaves (now his clients for life), his hired laborers, and sometimes business associates or tenants.

In Acts, and in the letters, too, we see the importance of the householder, or relatively well-to-do men and women who serve as patrons for the new communities. In this respect Christianity was like other clubs and associations, including synagogues. On the whole, however, the picture of the mission in Acts is much richer, grander, and more public than the picture that we can piece together from the letters. When E. A. Judge describes the Pauline group as "traveling Sophists or philosophers," accompanied by a "retinue" and supported by aristocratic patrons,[9] it is the picture from Acts that he is reflecting. One wonders how many Sophists and philosophers really traveled in so grand a style; certainly the impression we receive from Paul's letters is far less splendid. There, and from some details of the Acts account, we see communication more along natural networks of relationship, in each city and between cities. The families and houses of certain individuals were the starting points. In Corinth, Paul singles out the house of Stephanas as "the firstfruits of Achaia." The connections of work and trade were important, too.

In trying to imagine how the connections were made, we have to remember that the ancient city was quite small by our postindustrial standards. For example, Antioch in Syria was one of the real giants. It had between a quarter and a half-million inhabitants in the first century. Yet one could easily walk its circumference in an afternoon. The density was incredibly high—perhaps two hundred per acre, MacMullen estimates[10]—a density found today only in places like East Harlem and Calcutta. Such crowding was made tolerable by the spacious and elegant public areas and by a benign climate that permitted much life and business to be conducted in plazas and streets. There was, as a result, not much privacy. Not much that happened in a neighborhood would escape the eyes of the neighbors. News or rumor would travel rapidly. Words would quickly get around concerning the strange ceremonies and strange talk at that new Tentmakers' Club meeting over at Prisca and Aquila's house.

Just what was the new group like? To answer that question, we need to consider ways in which people formed groups and found identity in the ancient city. Several models were available that the Christians could follow, most of which I have already mentioned. First, there was the club—usually called *collegium* in Latin, *thiasos, synodos,* and other terms in Greek. Such voluntary associations multiplied in the Roman period. Most were small and had as their chief aim sociability, a convivial banquet with better-than-average wine once a month or so, and arrangements to insure a proper burial for each member when his or her time came. Civic associations of immigrants were exceptional among these clubs, often larger and more complex than the others. Among immigrant organizations, the synagogue of the Jews offered a particular model of voluntary group. Schools of rhetoric or of

[9] E. A. Judge, "The Early Christians as a Scholastic Community," *Journal of Religious History* 1 (1960): 125–35.
[10] MacMullen, p. 63.

philosophy offered another model. In some instances, the Epicureans and perhaps the Pythagoreans, the philosophical schools took on some of the characteristics of cultic associations. A number of scholars have suggested that the Pauline group could be considered a school in this strict sense. It is true that instruction in special beliefs and in standards of behavior expected of the enlightened was carried on by the Pauline leaders. It is true, too, that the letters of Paul contain many allusions to the sorts of topics that were currently under discussion in the schools, and even some features of school rhetoric can be found in the letters. Finally, the household itself, as I have already said, constituted the basic cell of the movement.

Each of these models exhibits important features that we can find in the early Christian group in the cities. There can be little doubt that these forms of socialization were well known to the Christians and had their influence on the way the Christian groups took shape. Yet there are also important differences in every case. No single model is adequate to explain the form that the urban congregations took, nor are all of them together a sufficient explanation of the character of the Christian *ekklēsia*. We have to entertain the possibility that the Christian movement in the cities, at its very beginning, invented a unique form of resocialization. Further, this resocialization may have been as important to the church's growth, effectiveness, and future nature as were its unique beliefs.

Space does not permit me to describe the novel form of socialization here. However, let me mention a few of the factors that helped the Pauline groups toward a special sense of cohesion. First, they made a clear distinction between insiders and outsiders. Boundaries were firmly marked. The Christian cult was exclusive in a way that no other Greco-Roman cult besides Judaism was. One could not be baptized into Christ and also intitiated into Lord Sarapis. One could not partake of the Table of Christ and the table of demons. Second, the Christians had a special language—not only an argot, but an argot that was particularly rich in the language of intimacy: "brother and sister," "love," "rejoicing," and other emotional language. Third, they shared peculiar beliefs, often stated in characteristic structures of language, like the antithetically parallel formulas about Christ's death and resurrection. Fourth, they learned a kind of theodicy that encompassed the hostility of outsiders ("the world"), anticipated it, and connected it with basic belief about the crucified messiah. Fifth, they developed ways of satisfying most social needs without going outside the community's own boundaries. In short, institutionalization began as soon as the first congregation was formed. Finally, they quickly developed peculiar, simple, but highly evocative rituals.

In all these ways, the community of Christians in each city developed as a tightly knit, self-conscious, disciplined group. At the same time it was different from other, similar groups in the city because Christians had a strange sense of being a supralocal fellowship. They had taken the Jewish notion of the people of God and the assembly of God, the *ekklēsia tou theou*, and adapted it to the facts of urban life in the imperial age in a special way. They came to think of themselves as a network of brothers and sisters spread across the world. Their structure would in time imitate the empire itself. Every time a traveling Christian from a distant province arrived with a letter of introduction and was welcomed as a sister or brother, the concept of that network took flesh. This special dialectic between the small, intimate, local group and the worldwide "town meeting of God" had unique potential. It may well be, as Adolf von Harnack said in a different context, that "it was this, and not any evangelist, which proved to be the most effective missionary."[11]

[11] Adolf von Harnack, *The Mission and Expansion of Christianity in the First Three Centuries*, trans. James Moffatt (Gloucester, Mass.: Peter Smith, 1972), p. 434.

3
Jerusalem: The City as Place

JONATHAN Z. SMITH
University of Chicago

In recent literature the theory of "place" involves a focus on the individual and his or her subjective experience, which transforms "place" to "home." One's place of birth may be accidental; but investing it with meaning, converting it into a home, is an act of human construction. This transformative act becomes a paradigm of all humane activity: the conversion of mere location into a locus of significance. To have a home is to have built.[1]

The centrality of "home" as the primary meaning of "place" has also led to modern theories of perceptual geography, which attempt to discern people's "mental maps"—particularly the mental maps of city folk. Studies on this subject began with the work of Charles Trowbridge in 1913, and have been continued by Kevin Lynch and Peter Gould in recent decades. Trowbridge was concerned with the interrelated questions of how children develop knowledge of geographic orientation and how adults negotiate unfamiliar urban terrain without disorientation. He discovered that both children and adults carry "imaginary maps" in their heads, which organize familiar terrain in relation to home. These maps are not street directions, but rather landmarks, feelings, memories which create a subjective landscape imposed on the objective organization of a neighborhood.

Trowbridge's notion of "imaginary maps" did not become a prime area of study until Kevin Lynch's influential *The Image of the City*, first published in 1960. In his book Lynch declared, "We must consider not just the city as a thing in itself, but the city as being perceived by its inhabitants."[2] Lynch was concerned also with Trowbridge's issue of orientation/disorientation. There are now a significant number of such studies, most devoted to present-day cities. There has even been some attempt to extend the techniques to past

---

[1] For a profound meditation on this theme, see Martin Heidegger, "Bauen, Wohnen, Denken," in *Vorträge und Aufsätze* (Pfullingen: G. Neske, 1954), pp. 145–62; *Martin Heidegger: Poetry, Language, Thought*, Albert Hofstadter, trans. (New York: Harper & Row, 1971), pp. 145–61.

[2] Kevin Lynch, *The Image of the City* (Cambridge: Harvard University Press, 1960), p. 3.

perception[3] and to imaginary cities in literature and utopian traditions.[4] With these studies has come increased sophistication of techniques and a closer rapprochement with the psychology of perception, perhaps best summarized in Peter Gould's work on "mental maps."[5] Place, from such a point of view, is essentially "inside" and therefore private, a view which makes it difficult to think of the city as place.

In contrast to the modern focus on individual perception, we must keep in mind the different implications of the classical theory: place is not created, it is given. Human beings seek their place, conform to their place, fulfill their place. They do so by keeping their place. From the classical point of view, place is neither individual nor egalitarian. Place is preeminently social and hierarchical. It is this understanding of "place" that informs the classical city.

On the subject of hierarchy, as distinct both from egalitarianism and individualism, and on its necessary presupposition of holism, Louis Dumont's *Homo Hierarchicus* is an excellent source.[6] I will refer to Dumont at some length below. Meanwhile, on the classical city as an expression of hierarchy in concrete form, I am indebted to Paul Wheatley's work, *The Pivot of the Four Corners*.[7]

In this work Wheatley has undertaken the most ambitious and careful comparative study of the origin of the city to date.[8] While focusing on urban origins on the North China Plain, he proposes an interpretation of data from the other six "regions of primary urban generation" as well: Mesopotamia, Egypt, the Indus Valley, Mesoamerica, the central Andes, and the Yoruba territories of southwestern Nigeria. After reviewing a number of factors proposed by scholars as central components in urban genesis (e.g., environment, demography, technology), he concludes that while each was a concomitant, they were not independent agents. The rise of the city, he says,

[3] For example, Brian W. Blouet and Merlin P. Lawson, eds., *Images of the Plains* (Lincoln: University of Nebraska Press, 1975), and H. R. Merrens, "The Physical Environment of Early America: Images and Image Makers in Colonial South Carolina," *Geographical Review* 59 (1969): 530–56.

[4] For example, C. S. Aiken, "Faulkner's Yoknapatawpha County: Geographical Fact into Fiction," *Geographical Review* 67 (1977): 1–12; P. W. Porter and F. E. Lukermann, "The Geography of Utopia," in David Lowenthal and Martyn J. Bowden, eds., *Geographies of the Mind* (New York: Oxford University Press, 1976), pp. 197–223.

[5] Peter R. Gould, *On Mental Maps* (Ann Arbor: University of Michigan, 1966) and Peter R. Gould and Rodney White, *Mental Maps* (Baltimore: Penguin Books, 1974).

[6] Louis Dumont, *Homo Hierarchichus: The Caste System and Its Implications*, rev. ed. (Chicago: University of Chicago Press, 1980). Abbreviated in text as *HH*.

[7] Paul Wheatley, *The Pivot of the Four Corners: A Preliminary Enquiry into the Origins and Character of the Ancient Chinese City* (Chicago: Aldine Pub. Co., 1971). Abbreviated in text as *PFC*. See also Wheatley's summary essay, *City as Symbol: An Inaugural Lecture*, University College London (London: H. K. Lewis, 1969).

[8] The only other major comparative effort I know of is that by Robert McC. Adams, *The Evolution of Urban Society: Early Mesopotamia and Prehispanic Mexico* (Chicago: Aldine Pub. Co., 1966).

is seen to be sustained by the concurrent emergence of a redistributive superordinate economy focused on the ceremonial complex. Such a change. . .presupposes the development of new social institutions. Indeed the questions it poses relate primarily to social differentiation. . . . (PFC 267,281)

The primary form of social differentiation in the formation of classical cities, Wheatley suggests, was the emergence of specialized priests (as opposed to the later kings). Religion provided the ideological grounds for the hierarchical restructuring of society. Among the chief innovations of the city were those centered on "those branches of technology concerned with ritual display" (PFC 305).

I found Wheatley's notion of the city as a ceremonial complex extremely provocative, although he has an overly instrumental understanding of ritual. This error is corrected, while his thesis is richly amplified, in a recent study by Clifford Geertz titled, *Negara: The Theatre State in Nineteenth Century Bali*.[9] In this book Geertz argues:

> The expressive nature of the Balinese state was apparent through the whole of its known history, for it was always pointed not toward. . . government, which it pursued indifferently and hesitantly, but rather toward spectacle, toward ceremony, toward the public dramatization of the ruling obsessions of Balinese culture: social inequality and status pride. It was a theatre state in which the kings and princes were the impresarios, the priests the directors, and the peasants the supporting cast, stage crew, and audience. (NTSB 13)

Later in the study, Geertz expands the argument as follows:

> The state cult was not a cult of the state. It was an argument, made over and over again in the insistent vocabulary of ritual, that worldly status has a cosmic base, that hierarchy is the governing principle of the universe. . . . [This is] the point that the state ceremonies made: Status is all. (NTSB 102)

In this essay I should like to elaborate on the relationship of city, hierarchy, and the technology of ritual with respect to a single city—Jerusalem—as it appears in sections of two Jewish and two Christian sources. In doing so, I will make explicit use of insights afforded by Wheatley, Geertz, and Louis Dumont.

In *Homo Hierarchicus*[10] Louis Dumont makes a major contribution to social theory by insisting on an absolute distinction between status and power. Status is relative, he argues, and refers to a hierarchy of degrees of purity and impurity, with the priest at its summit. It is essentially a sacerdotal system. Power, on the other hand, is a matter of dominance, a hier-

---

[9] Clifford Geertz, *Negara: The Theatre State in Nineteenth Century Bali* (Princeton: Princeton University Press, 1980). Abbreviated in text as *NTSB*.
[10] See note 6, above.

archy of degrees of legitimate force, with the king at its summit. It is essentially a juridical system. The two systems exhibit a necessary complementarity. The king will always be impure with respect to the priest, but the priest's authority will be inferior with respect to the king. The priest legitimates the power of the king; the king supports, protects, and preserves the status of the priest.

There is no doubt, in Dumont, that the opposition pure/impure is to be associated with a hierarchy of status and with the priestly function. It is less clear that Dumont would formulate the distinction sacred/profane as a hierarchy of power, to be associated with the royal function. That association seems to me, however, the clear implication of his few statements on this theme. The relationship between the two systems seems to be part of Old Testament priestly speculative tradition, as represented by Ezekiel 40–48, a possibility specifically allowed for by Dumont (*HH* 365). This passage in Ezekiel, therefore, will be the first of my four sources for discussion of Jerusalem as a city of hierarchy and ritual.

Ezekiel 40–48, along with the "Temple Scroll" from Qumran and Mishnah, provides the clearest articulated hierarchical ideology of the temple as the defining element in Jerusalem. For the purpose of this discussion, I am concerned with the social reality of the temple, i.e., the mapping of social configurations. In these chapters of Ezekiel social mapping is focused on the temple rather than the city. Thus we find the first item in the introductory vision: "the hand of the Lord. . . set me down on a very high mountain on which was a structure like a city [i.e., the temple] opposite me."[11] The city recurs in the later division of territories (Ezek. 45.6 and 48.15–20), but only as a residual category.

To use Dumont's terminology, I would argue that there are four homologous maps in Ezekiel 40–48. The first (Ezek. 40–44.3) is a hierarchy of *power* built on the dichotomy of sacred/profane. The second (Ezek. 44.4–31) is a hierarchy of *status* built on the dichotomy of pure/impure. The third map (Ezek. 45.1–8 and 47.13–48.35) is *territorial*, and the fourth (Ezek. 46) is predominantly *orientational*. These latter two are isomorphic to the first map.[12]

It is beyond the scope of this essay to lay out all four maps and correlate fully the architectural with the social details. For here, as in Geertz's descrip-

[11] I have followed, with occasional emendation, the translation of the Revised Standard Version. For the details with which this essay is concerned, the older commentary by George A. Cooke, *A Critical and Exegetical Commentary on the Book of Ezekiel* (Edinburgh: T & T Clark, 1936), pp. 425–531, has proven more useful than the more recent and more "theological" commentaries I have also consulted, such as Walther Zimmerli, *Ezechiel* (Neukirchen: Neukirchener Verlag, 1955–69) and Walter Eichrodt, *Ezekiel* (London: Students Christian Movement Press, 1970).

[12] In distinguishing these maps, I make no assumptions as to literary traditions. On these, see Hartmut Gese, *Der Verfassungsentwurf des Ezechiel (Kap. xl–xlviii): Traditionsgeschichtlich Untersucht* (Tübingen: Mohr, 1957) and Zimmerli, pp. 976–1249.

tion of the palace as temple in Bali, the social and ideological distinctions are "cast in a vocabulary of walls, gates, passageways, sheds and furniture" (*NTSB* 109). Rather, I shall focus only on the specifically anthropological details in the first two maps: Ezek. 40–44.3, which I designate a hierarchy of power; and Ezek. 44.4–31, which I designate a hierarchy of status. That is to say, I shall focus on kings, Zadokites, Levites, people and foreigners, in respect to gross spatial categories (outer court, inner court, etc.), and not on the fine architectural detail.

From one point of view, the first map (the hierarchy of power) makes only one distinction, that between the sacred and the profane. "This is the law of the temple: the whole territory round about the top of the mountain shall be most holy. Behold, this is the law of the temple" (43.12). With respect to that which is "down the mountain" or "off the mountain" (i.e., the profane), the top of the mountain is the undifferentiated sacred. From another point of view, if one focuses only on the top of the mountain, an analogous and more detailed set of differentia can be established.

At the center is the "most holy place." It is restricted to YHWH, his "glory" and his angels—the place of the royal function of the deity (41.3–4). It is his "throne-place" (43.7). Note here the typical replication within sacred/profane hierarchies: as the temple mount is the most holy place in relation to the rest of the land, so YHWH's royal space is the most holy place in relation to the rest of the temple. This space is capable of endless segmentation. As the wall described in Ezek. 42.20 makes plain, the temple as a whole is sacred with respect to the rest of the temple mount, and so on. That is to say, with respect to the temple mount, the land is profane; with respect to the temple, the temple mount is profane; with respect to the "throne-place," the temple is profane. These distinctions are reinforced by the fact that we are not to picture them as concentric circles on a flat plane. Each unit is built on a terrace, spatially higher than the unit which it surpasses in holiness (40.20–49).

The actors in the ritual drama of the temple are arranged accordingly. They operate in different spheres of relative sacrality, ranked in relations of power. Thus most proximate to the "throne-place" is the "holy place," the sphere of the Zadokite priests. (42.14). They are "in charge of the altar," they alone may "come near to YHWH to minister to him" (40.46), they eat the "most holy offerings" dedicated to YHWH (42.13); if they leave their proper sphere they must change their garments (which have become holy) so as not to endanger those of lesser status (42.14). The next sphere (moving outwards and downwards) is that of the temple, the realm of the "priests who have charge of the temple" (40.45). And finally, there is "that which is for the people" (42.14).

Up to this point, Ezek. 40–44.3 represents a classical hierarchy of power arranged in terms of sacred/profane and expressed, spatially, by the relative distance of each rank from the center, as well as the relative height of their domain. But there is more. The system is perturbed by a conflict at the level of power. If the priest is clearly subordinate to YHWH (the highest ranked priest ministers to him), what about the Israelite king? This question is especially acute within that Israelite ideology that concentrates the royal function on YHWH.

According to Dumont's definitions, hierarchy of status gives theoretical grounds for the subordination of the king in terms of the dichotomy pure/impure. Thus the first map breaks with its power system and introduces the vocabulary of status with an idiom of pure/impure to explain how the king relates to the temple. Ezek. 43.4–9 is the decisive passage. The kings (and through them, the people) have polluted the temple by their actions, particularly by burying dead kings on the temple mount, thus introducing corpse pollution.[13] They have also put the royal palace adjacent to YHWH's palace (the temple) "with only a wall between me and them," setting "their threshold by my threshold and their doorposts by my doorposts." The solution to the first problem is given in this passage: let them put "the dead bodies of their kings far from me."

The solution to the second problem is given in the first verses of Ezek. 44, which both content and literary analysis show belong to the first map. That is, they conclude chapter 43 rather than introduce chapter 44.

> Then he [the angel] brought me back towards the outer gate of the sanctuary which faces east and it was shut. Then YHWH[14] said to me: This gate is to remain shut. It shall not be opened, and no one shall enter by it; for YHWH, the God of Israel, has entered by it, therefore it shall remain shut. Only the king, only he alone,[15] may sit in it in order to take bread before YHWH. He shall enter by way of the vestibule of the gate and shall go out by the same way. (44.1–3)

It would appear at first glance that the king is being given special status. He has access to the vestibule of the outer, eastern gateway which is reserved for YHWH alone. No other human being has such access. Hence Eichrodt: "the one person counted worthy of treading on such a holy spot is the reigning prince of Israel." [16] The king's access, however, is from the opposite direction. He does not enter from the (solar) east, but from the (dark) west—the

---

[13] I am aware of the argument by D. Neiman, "Canaanite Cult Object in the Old Testament," *Journal of Biblical Literature* 67 (1948): 55–60, that *pgr* can be translated as "stelae." Note the contrast to Christian cathedrals where corpses of kings and martyrs confer sanctity, as is discussed in Peter Brown, *The Cult of the Saints* (Chicago: University of Chicago Press, 1981), pp. 4–6, and *passim*. But this is hierarchy of power, not of status.

[14] Most editors emend the Hebrew text at this point and substitute "he [the angel]" for YHWH. But if it is YHWH who announces the problem in Ezek 43.6, then it is YHWH who here gives the solution. The least of the problems with Ezekiel is having YHWH speak of himself in the third person!

[15] Literally, "only the prince, the prince, may sit in it" (Ezek. 44.3).

[16] Eichrodt, p. 560.

only one of the four cardinal directions that has no gate. This detail suggests that the king is no king, but rather a mock king, as one might find in a saturnalian role reversal. The king's putative special status turns out to be the very underside of YHWH's royalty. Furthermore, by limiting the king's sphere of activity to the gate house of the outer gateway which opens into the outer court, the king appears to be excluded from the temple proper. To invoke, anachronistically, the scheme of later temple maps, the king's sphere can be compared to the Court of the Gentiles, the public, civic space of the temple.[17]

The second map, Ezek. 44.4–31, is a hierarchy of status constructed on the idiom of pure/impure. The overall topic is well captured by the Revised Standard Version's paraphrastic recasting of the obscure Hebrew: "those who may be admitted to the temple and all those who are to be excluded from the sanctuary." In this map the king is not figured.

The utterly impure are the foreigners, those "uncircumcised in heart and flesh." They "profane" the temple and the sacrifices. They are to be totally excluded (44.7,9). What is most interesting about this otherwise unexceptional classification is that it is presented as an innovation. Formerly, such foreigners were employed within the sanctuary as temple slaves (44.8). In a stunning shift, interpreted as "punishment," the Levites are now to assume this role.

Within the temple, there is an ascending hierarchy of purity of the ritual actors. At the lowest rung are the people, about whom no details are given (44.19). Next are the Levites, who can pollute, but for whom no purity regulations are given (44.10–14). At the summit are the Zadokites, for whom detailed purity regulations are given as to dress and marriage rules, corpse and carrion avoidance (44.15–31).

The hierarchy of status may also be expressed in spatial idiom. The people are confined to the other court. The Levites range from the gates through the temple, but "they shall not come near me, serve me as priest, nor come near any of my sacred things and the things that are most sacred." The Zadokites have the greatest spatial range; they "enter" YHWH's space and "approach his table," but they also "go out into the outer court to the people" (44.10–31).

As a striking contrast to the maps we have been considering in Ezekiel, let us look at the description of Judaea in Aristeas' *Letter to Philocrates* 83–121.[18] Aristeas provides a picture of a well-ordered state, dominated by its capital city, which in turn is dominated by the temple. But this "domination"

---

[17] Cf. Ezek 46.1–13 for a somewhat different elaboration of the king's role.

[18] The text I am referring to is established by André Pelletier, *Lettre d'Aristée à Philocrates*, Sources Chrétiennes 89 (Paris: Editions du Cerf, 1962); abbreviated as *LP*. The English translation is by Moses Hadas, *Aristeas to Philocrates* (New York: Ktav Pub. House, 1951).

is not hierarchical. There are no indications of status, no degrees of purity/ impurity; there is almost nothing in the way of rank.[19] Perhaps this may be attributed to the author's apparent lack of firsthand acquaintance with the city, to his imitation of hellenistic utopian ethnographies, or to his self-conscious deparochialization of Jewish religious traditions.[20] But the contrast remains and may be seen as conceptual rather than idiosyncratic. Aristeas understands Jerusalem primarily as part of a political, not a religious system. He depicts Jerusalem as exemplary civic space, a cosmopolitan capital, though somewhat small by Alexandrian standards.

In Aristeas' picture, the periphery of Judaea is completely encircled by mountains which supply natural defenses (*LP* 118), and surrounded by the river Jordan, which rises annually and irrigates the fields (116). The countryside is primarily agricultural (112), and is arranged, checkerboard fashion, in equal-size lots (116). At its center, situated on a high mountain (83), is a *polis*, described with extreme brevity (105–6). At the center of the city, at its highest point (84), stands the temple. No expense has been spared in its construction (85). Its sewer system is especially noteworthy (88–91). Within the temple, sacrifices are carried on in silence by some seven hundred well-ordered and industrious priests. There is no explanation as to why sacrifices are being performed, no suggestion of various ranks of priests or regions of the temple, no indication of any separation between priests and laity, no suggestion that anyone is forbidden access to the temple or its precincts (92–95). Aristeas ascribes more sense of separation and awe to the citadel (102–4), where entry is a matter of military security, than to the temple. The high priest is introduced as a figure of sovereignty, rather than purity (96–99). His major function in the narrative is to discourse on the ecological elements determining the optimum size of cities (112).

It should now be possible to summarize the crucial differences between Ezekiel and the letter of Aristeas, as regards maps of hierarchy. In Ezekiel, by employing a hierarchy of status alongside the hierarchy of power, the system can be endlessly replicated both within the temple complex and without. Lacking the presence of a king, or even the promise of one, the hierarchy of status remains in place; though the hierarchy of power may be adjusted or abandoned. Whether expressed in the simple Wisdom poem of Isa. 28.23–29 or in the complex exfoliation of Mishnah, the hierarchy of status does not need to be centralized in the temple. In contrast the capital/ countryside, center/periphery model employed by Aristeas cannot be de-centralized. His understanding cannot survive the destruction of the temple or the political disenfranchisement of Jerusalem. Not only is the model

---

[19] There is only one opaque reference, that people, when on the streets, are careful not to make contact, "so that those in a state of purity may touch nothing improper" (Hadas, p. 106).

[20] *Ibid.*, pp. 139–66. The idiom of pure/impure, which is most dense in this passage, refers solely to virtues and social relations.

flawed in principle by being indeterminate "at the fringes,"[21] but it is tied inextricably to geopolitical history. It is not systemic and replicable; it is historical, hence unrepeatable.

At this juncture we can begin a discussion of the Christian materials on Jerusalem. They are tied to the historical, but in a fashion different from Aristeas. They are also tied to a hierarchy of power, but never, to my knowledge, to one of status. When discussing ritual and hierarchy in Christian cities, one thinks immediately of Constantinople. The "new Rome" was deliberately crafted as a stage for Christian imperial and sacred ritual. One remembers also the later elaboration of Byzantine ritual, employing all the elements of this stage, as memorialized in works such as *De ceremoniis aulae byzantinae* of Constantine VII. The Jerusalem of Eusebius, who wrote about it in his *Life of Constantine,* has proven in many ways as interesting.

We no longer have Eusebius's treatise on the Church of the Holy Sepulchre in Jerusalem (if it was ever written), nor do we have a lengthy panegyric for that church as we do for the church at Tyre. But the brief description of the site and construction of the Jerusalem church in Eusebius's *Vita Constantini* 3.25–40 is perhaps all the more valuable for its highly compressed character.[22]

To summarize Eusebius's account: Constantine, under divine guidance, addressed himself to constructing a building at the site of the resurrection in Jerusalem. "He deemed it necessary to bring to light . . . the blessed place . . . so that all might be able to see and venerate it" (*VC* 3.25). But there was a problem: the spot was buried under rubble and dirt. We would describe this as the result of a landfill project, which had been undertaken to provide the foundation for the vast Hadrianic urban renewal project of Aeila Capitolina. Eusebius described it differently. The "world race of demons" through the instrumentality of "impious men" and "atheists" sought to place in "darkness [and] oblivion" that spot marked by the "light of the angel who had descended from heaven" as described in Matt. 28.3. This they did by "piling up earth brought there from elsewhere," and by covering the packed dirt fill with paving stones. (*VC* 3.26). Note that Eusebius intends us to understand these actions, not as part of an overall civil engineering project, but as premediated attacks taken specifically against one particular *topos*.

The language Eusebius uses in this introductory narrative is the language of cosmogonic myth. A bit later in the text, Constantine is made to say

---

[21] This problem plagues contemporary geographical and urban sociological discussions of the urban center/urban fringe. See Raymond E. Pahl, ed., *Readings in Urban Sociology* (Oxford and New York: Pergamon Press, 1968), pp. 263–97, for a review of the literature.

[22] For the text of the *Vita Constantini,* abbreviated as *VC,* I have used Ivar August Heikel, *Eusebius Werke,* Griechische Christliche Schriftsteller (Leipzig: J. C. Heinrichs, 1902), 1: 1–148, esp. pp. 89–95. English translation found in *The Greek Ecclesiastical Historians of the First Six Centuries of the Christian Era* (London, 1845), 6: 1–234, esp. 136–47, which I cite with considerable emendation.

that the place has been holy *ex arches* (*VC* 3.30). It was a place once marked
by light; demonic forces plunged the light into darkness; now the place, once
more, through the agency of the king, is brought into light. This is the
fundamental royal cosmogony—concerned, in Theodore Gaster's term, with
the revival or renewal of the "topocosm" after a period of chaos.[23]

After this mythic passage, Eusebius shifts his language again, this time
to the idiom of pure/impure. For, after covering the site, the demons built a
temple and altar to Aphrodite, a "licentious demon," above the tomb. On
her "profane altar" were offered "polluted sacrifices," making the place one
of "abominations." Constantine, again acting under divine guidance, ordered a *katharsis* of these "impurities" and "pollutions." Aphrodite's temple
and altar were torn down (*VC* 3.26). But more was required. The stones and
timbers that had made up the temple were "carted far out into the countryside," the ground underneath the temple was dug up to a considerable
depth, and likewise carted away (*VC* 3.27). Although Constantine does not
perform these acts, he is functioning as a priest, having the polluting elements removed from a sacred place.

We might compare this brief scene with the scenario for purifying the
polluted temple of Jerusalem in 2 Chron. 29.3–19. Here the king (Hezekiah),
commands the priest and Levites to "sanctify the house of YHWH. . . and
carry out the filth from the holy place." The priests cleansed the temple, and
"brought out all the uncleanness which they found in the temple," and
placed it in the temple court. The Levites then "took it and carried it out to
the brook Kidron." Then they reported to the king that the temple had been
cleansed. In this narrative, there is a clear, hierarchical division of labor. The
king, as guardian and patron of the temple, commands its purification and
pays for the restoration of its outer form: "he [Hezekiah] opened the
doors. . . and repaired them." But the priests are the specialists in pollution
and its removal. The other major cleansing incident associated with the
temple is less clear in its hierarchy—perhaps because, under the Maccabees, functions are more blurred. In 1 Maccabees, Judas, acting as a king,
"chose blameless priests devoted to the law and they cleansed the sanctuary
and removed the defiled stones to an unclean place" (1 Macc. 4.42–43).[24] In
2 Maccabees, the purification is performed by Judas and his followers, not by
priests (2 Macc. 10.2–3). In Josephus, the purification of the temple is
undertaken in private by Judas alone.[25]

---

[23] Theodor H. Gaster, *Thespis*, rev. ed. (Garden City, N.Y.: Doubleday, 1961), p. 17 and
passim.
[24] The problem of the altar stones and their removal and reservation on the temple mount
(4. 44–46) appears to reflect a difficult problem in purity regulations. See J. A. Goldstein, *I
Maccabees* (Garden City, N.Y.: Doubleday, 1976), p. 285, although rabbinic materials
cannot be brought to bear.
[25] Josephus, *Antiquities* 12. 318. The text and translation cited here are the 8 vol. Loeb
Library edition, trans. H. Thackery and R. Marcus (Cambridge: Harvard University
Press, 1934).

Eusebius's narrative returns to the language of myth, now correlating the generic myth of a renewed creation as the emergence from demonic darkness with the specifically Christian myth of the resurrection. For, after removing the polluted earth, "Behold! The place which had witnessed the resurrection of the Savior reappeared, surpassing all hopes." The grave itself was resurrected. The "Holy of Holies" rose to light, "in a manner strikingly similar to the raising up of the Savior" (VC 3.28).

Now, having played the mythic-heroic role of king, and the cleansing role of priest, Constantine reverts to the more human role of king in relation to the temple. He becomes its chief patron, devoting money to the construction and adornment of the new church building (VC 3.29 and 40).

The remainder of the narrative is primarily concerned with the architectural details of the new building, save for one striking new note. The Church of the Holy Sepulchre, already referred to as the "Holy of Holies" and as having been built on a "spot holy ex arches," is to be the new temple of the new Christian Jerusalem. It is a "new Jerusalem face to face with the old." It will be "that second new Jerusalem spoken of by the prophet" (VC 3.33).

Eusebius invites us to compare the Constantinian church foundation with the temple in Jerusalem. We should accept the invitation. There is nothing inherent in the location of the temple in Jerusalem. The location is simply where it "happened" to be built. There are indeed other shrines, often rivals to Jerusalem, for which aetiological materials have been transmitted. Bethel would be the most obvious example, both for its name, "House of God," and its identification with a significant event in the life of a patriarch—an event which expresses several of the central ideological features of temple. But there is no aitia for the location of Jerusalem's temple. It was built as a royal prerogative at a place of royal choosing. Its power, relative to the populace and to other shrines, was maintained or reduced by the imperium. The temple in Jerusalem was the focus of a self-referential system. It could have been built anywhere else and still have been the same. It requires no rationale beyond the obvious one that, having been declared a temple, it becomes, by being so established, a place of clarification—most particularly of the hierarchical rules and roles of sacred/profane, purity/impurity. In an apparent paradox, its arbitrariness guarantees its ordering role. There is nothing to distract from the system. Later Jewish traditions will develop a complex mythology of the temple site and its "stone of foundation" stretching from creation to final redemption, but this is only developed in the absence of temple, king, and priest. Under such conditions, the temple needs legitimation, needs to be perceived as not arbitrary, precisely because it no longer plays an ordering role. It is no accident that the mythology developed for the temple in these later materials correspond in many details to that developed in Christianity for Golgotha.[26]

Christianity had the opposite situation. A Constantinople could be arbitrary and, hence, highly systematized. But what of Jerusalem or Galilee? The Church of the Holy Sepulchre could not be built anywhere else and still be the same. It was tied to the sacred biography of the Savior. While the site of the birth, crucifixion, and resurrection have immediate power—hence their elaboration into a cosmic mythology—any place mentioned in the gospels or hagiographies could, in principle, become the site of a memorial or commemorative church. This, the vast literature of Christian pilgrimage makes plain.

Aristeas informs us that the temple in Jerusalem was a silent cult. "Complete silence prevails, so that one may suppose that not a person was present in the place" (*LP* 95). All was system, a series of hierarchic and hieratic transactions of sacred/profane, pure/impure. Each transaction was a focus of all transactions; each transaction was capable of endless replication. In short, it was a system of synchrony. But there is another mode of order, a diachronic one of narrative and story, which is liturgy.

Since the pioneering researches of Baumstark, it is well established that, due in no small part to pilgrimage, the liturgy of Jerusalem had a decisive role in the development of liturgical practices in both the East and West.[27] This is not surprising, for in Jerusalem gesture and story could be brought together in a unique fashion. Any homiletician could develop the general typology: "After these things you were led to the holy pool of divine baptism, as Christ was carried from the Cross to the Sepulchre . . ."; but no one, except a Cyril in Jerusalem could add, ". . . from the Cross to the Sepulchre *which is before our eyes.*"[28] Story and place were one. Beyond Cyril, the liturgy of Jerusalem must be recovered from other, later rites (the Old Armenian, the Old Georgian, the Old Palestinian Melkite and the Old Iberian), with one exception, the mid-fifth century *Pilgrimage of Egeria.*[29]

The first part in Egeria's text, the itinerary (*P* 1–23), is dominated by *loci:* "this is the place where" some scriptural event occurred; "this is the place according to scriptures"; "this the place called" by scripture. It is what we would expect in a pilgrim text, the scripture as a *Guide bleu.* But there is also the clear notion of a link between a particular passage and a particular place before which one stands—the *aptus locus* (*P* 4.4), the *pertinens ad rem* (*P* 10.7). In this we see the distinctive contribution of place to the birth of Christian liturgy, as opposed to dominical instruction and general (largely

---

[27] Anton Baumstark, *Comparative Liturgy,* rev. by Bernard Botte, trans. F. L. Cross (Westminster, Md: Newman Press, 1958), p. 6.

[28] Cyril of Jerusalem, *Mystagogical Catacheses* 2.4. Text and trans. in Frank L. Cross, *Saint Cyril of Jerusalem's Lectures on the Christian Sacraments* (Crestwood, N.Y.: St. Vladimir's Press, 1977), pp. 19, 60.

[29] The text used is Otto Prinz, ed. *Itinerarium Egeriae,* 5th edition, *Sammlung Vulgarlateinischer Texte* (Heidelberg, 1960), abbreviated as *P.* The English translation is by G. E. Gingras, *Egeria: Diary of the Pilgrimage,* Ancient Christian Writers 38 (New York: Newman Press, 1970).

Jewish) patterns of celebration. This link takes a fixed form in the *Pilgrimage:* the pilgrim arrives at a place noteworthy in scripture, a prayer is said, followed by the reading of a biblical (usually Pentateuchal) passage "proper" to the place, then a psalm fitting to the place, concluded by a final prayer (*P* 4.3; 10.4–7; 11.3; 12.3, etc.). When viewing other Christian memorials, the same general pattern would be followed with the appropriate lectionary substitutions: thus passages concerning Saint Thomas at his church at Edessa, "the complete acts of Saint Thecla" at her church outside of Seleucia of Isauria (*P* 19.2; 23.5). In this manner, story, liturgical action, and the immediate presence of a unique place are brought into juxtaposition. One example may serve for the rest.

> He [the bishop at Carrhae, formerly Harran] immediately guided us to the church which is outside the city, on the very spot where the house of Abraham stood, built on the very foundations and with the very stones of the house, so the saintly bishop said. After we had entered the church, a prayer was said, and the proper passage was read from Genesis. A Psalm was sung, another prayer was said, and after the bishop had blessed us, we went outside. Then he graciously agreed to guide us to the well from which the holy woman Rebecca had drawn water. (*P* 20.3)

The first section, despite all its arduous movement, proceeds at a leisurely pace: the finding of this or that *locus*, being endlessly shown "all the places I was always seeking out following the scriptures" (*P* 1.1; 5.12; 6.2, etc.). In part this is because the places themselves are rather thinly or accidentally distributed. A density of significance is found only in the valley at the base of Mount Sinai. Here significance becomes *de trop*, and the pilgrim is overwhelmed.

> And so we were shown everything written in the holy books of Moses that was done there in that valley . . . It was too much, however, to write down each one individually, because so many details could not be retained. (*P* 5.8)

How much more so in Jerusalem! Here is a plenitude of signification which, if reported in every detail, would simply result in confusion.

In this context a formal, liturgical ordering occurs, establishing a hierarchy of significance which focuses attention, primarily by adding a temporal dimension. The pilgrim is free to be at whatever place he or she wishes to see, at whatever time; the celebrant must be at a fixed place at a fixed time to perform a fixed act which focuses the intended significance of this conjunction.

Hence, to move from the first part of the *Pilgrimage* to the second, the description of the liturgical practices of Jerusalem (*P* 24–49), is to move from the leisurely to the highly determined. All is done *per ordinem*, "in a

prescribed manner"; everything is *consuetudinem*, "what is customary." [30]
The concern for appropriateness continues, but no longer, as for the pilgrim,
in terms of *apta loco;* for the celebrant it is *apta diei* (P 25.11; 35.4), or,
continuing the special advantage of Jerusalem, *apta diei et loco* (P 32.1; 35.2;
36.1, etc.).

In the second part of the *Pilgrimage*, the vast daily, weekly, and annual
drama of the liturgical year is spread forth. Each element specifies a day and
time (generalizable) as well as a particular place (unique to Jerusalem). With
few exceptions, [31] the hymns, prayers, scripture lessons, and gestures tied to
particular places in the Jerusalem liturgy can be exported. The sequence of
time (the story, the festal calendar) has allowed a supercession of place. It is
the *apta diei* which will be endlessly replicable, rather than the *apta loco*.

The structured temporality of the Christian liturgy accomplished for
Jerusalem and its churches what the Jewish hierarchical structures accomplished for Jerusalem and its temple. Both structures (being structures, and
hence replicable) could become independent of place—independent objects
of thought and creativity for which the destructive events of 70, 135, 614 or
637 C.E. were irrelevant. These different structures were condensed for the
one tradition in Mishnah, for the other, in the liturgical year. Each of these
enduring monuments is a "new Jerusalem."[32]

---

[30] Willem van Oorde, *Lexicon Aetherianum* (Amsterdam: H. J. Paris, 1930), pp. 41–42,
145.

[31] As described in the text, the Palm Sunday ritual, which is a reenactment of the
entrance into Jerusalem, cannot be "exported" (P 31). There are other, more minor
examples, e.g. P 39, 5—perhaps the most intensively local passage in the liturgical
description.

[32] A much expanded form of this essay will be published by the University of Chicago
Press, under the title, *In Search of Place: Towards a Theory of Ritual*.

4

Alien Citizens: A Marvelous Paradox

ROWAN GREER
Yale Divinity School

The letter to Diognetus, written by an unknown hand probably in the second century, purports to be a Christian response to pagan curiosity about a cult which enables its adherents both "to set. . . little store by this world, and even to make light of death itself" and to display a "warm fraternal affection" for one another. In chapter five of the letter the Christian stance toward earthly cities is described as a marvelous paradox:

> Though they are residents at home in their own countries, their behavior there is more like that of transients; they take their full part as citizens, but they also submit to anything and everything as if they were aliens. For them, any foreign country is a homeland, and any homeland a foreign country.[1]

The writer points to the fact that Christians, though in most respects no different from others, have renounced certain widespread practices of the Roman world. For example, "they marry and beget children, though they do not expose their infants." More profoundly, they exemplify the Pauline paradox of strength perfected in weakness (2 Cor. 6.1–10; 12.5–10). The letter to Diognetus suggests that Christians bear the same relation to the world that the soul does to the body. Diffused throughout the cities of the world, Christians are in one sense imprisoned and rejected by them, but also hold those cities together and remind them of a heavenly destiny.

The marvelous paradox of Christians as alien citizens is one that finds roots in the New Testament and constant expression in the writings of the early Church.[2] And yet to find a precise way of defining the paradox—either as a theory or as a description of practice—is a frustrating task. The letter to Diognetus scarcely supplies us with an elaborated theory. And, since the document is bereft of any certain social setting, we have no way of under-

[1] *The Epistle to Diognetus* 5.4, *The Apostolic Fathers*, trans. Kirsopp Lake (Cambridge: Harvard University Press, 1959), 2: 358.

[2] Representative passages in the New Testament include: Gal. 4.26, Phil. 3.20, Heb. 12.22, 1 Pet. 2.11, and Rev. 21–22.

standing the practice to which the author alludes, save to imagine in very general terms what it might have been like to be a Christian in a Roman city in the second century.

But the problem for Christians transcends understanding the letter to Diognetus. To define the paradox, to consider how to practice it, was and continues to be the task of Christians at all times and in all places. In what follows I should like briefly to examine the theme of alien citizenship as it appears in select but representative writers in two rather different contexts: the ante-Nicene church, and the imperial church of the fourth century.

I. The Ante-Nicene Church

The church of the first three centuries displays a bewildering inconsistency in its stance toward the culture around it. One thinks of the martyr Polycarp, confident of a higher judgment than Caesar's, dismissing a crowd by saying in irony, "Away with the atheists!" But one also thinks of Origen explaining Christianity in the salon of a pagan dowager empress. The Roman government was sometimes regarded as the obscene beast of Revelation, sometimes as an order in which Christians had a stake. They were proud of their aristocratic martyrs and magnified (when they did not invent) their share in supporting the empire. The Christians of the Thundering Legion had preserved Marcus Aurelius's army under duress. And it was this same philosopher-king to whom Melito of Sardis addressed his claim that Christianity, which began in the reign of Augustus, was "an omen of good to your empire, for from that time the power of the Romans became great and splendid."[3] Tertullian of Carthage and Clement of Alexandria, both writing in the early third century, seem to represent the two poles of the early church's inconsistency. Tertullian tends to reject the Roman world; Clement, to embrace it. While there is truth to this conclusion, a closer look will demonstrate that both begin by seeking to understand the marvelous paradox of alien citizenship.

Tertullian addresses his *Apology* to the rulers of the Roman Empire. He begins by noting that truth—to be understood, of course, as Christianity— "knows she is but a sojourner on the earth, and that among strangers she naturally finds foes."[4] The strangers, however, are not necessarily foes; and

---

[3] Eusebius, *Historia Ecclesiae* 4.26.7, *The Ecclesiastical History*, trans. Kirsopp Lake (Cambridge: Harvard University Press, 1959), 1, 389.

[4] Tertullian, *Apology* 1, ANF 3.17. Quotations from the early church fathers are cited using the following abbreviations:

> ANF: *The Ante-Nicene Christian Library: Translations of the writings of the Fathers down to A.D. 325*, ed. Alexander Roberts and James Donaldson (Edinburgh: 1866–72. American reprint, rev. by A. Cleveland Coxe, Grand Rapids: Wm. B. Eerdmans, 1969–71).
>
> NPNF 1, 2: Series One and Two, *A Select Library of Nicene and Post-Nicene Fathers of the Christian Church*, ed. Philip Schaff and Henry Wace (New York: The Christian Literature Company, 1886–1900).

Abbreviated titles of particular works are cited in the text with book, chapter, and verse; followed by volume and page of *ANF*, or series, volume, and page of *NPNF*.

what Tertullian says has the possibility of being construed as a statement of the marvelous paradox. Christians, though aliens, can also be Romans who benefit the empire and its cities. At least this is where Tertullian begins:

> We. . . are accused of being useless in the affairs of life. How in all the world can that be the case with people who are living among you, eating the same food, wearing the same attire, having the same habits, under the same necessities of existence? We are not Indian Brahmins or Gymnosophists, who dwell in woods and exile themselves from ordinary human life. (*Apol.* 57, ANF 3.49)

Christians participate in the economic and social life of the empire and benefit it as much as anyone else. Moreover, by their behavior they actively support the moral order of society. Though wrongly accused of infanticide, they alone do not expose their children. It is the pagans who stand convicted of the very crimes they seek to fasten on Christians (*Apol.* 8–9; *Ad Nationes* 15–16, ANF 3). Tertullian's claim is that, since no one is truly a Christian who fails to meet the moral demands of his or her faith, "we. . . alone are without crime" (*Apol.* 45, ANF 3.50). Not only has "virtue put some restraint on the world's wickedness," but Christian prayers have also averted God's wrath and mitigated disaster (*Apol.* 40, ANF 3.48; *To Scapula* 4, ANF 3.106f.). Finally, the Christian sojourners pray for the strangers' empire, because in God's providence it has been ordained to restrain evil and to delay the end of the world.

While Tertullian recognizes that Christians are a part of society, his emphasis is upon the other side of the paradox: the strangers amongst whom Christians live often turn out to be foes. He connects the rapid growth of the church to this opposition. Indeed, he goes so far as to claim that Christians now come close to constituting "the majority in every city" (*To Scapula* 2, ANF 3.106).[5] "We are but of yesterday, and we have filled every place among you—cities, islands, fortresses, towns, marketplaces, the very camp, tribes, companies, palace, senate, forum—we have left nothing to you but the temples of your gods" (*Apol.* 37, ANF 3.45). Even if we discount Tertullian's rhetoric, the impression remains that Christianity was a growing and alien power within ancient society. The reaction of pagans in Tertullian's day was no different than in the time of Nero. Christians were regarded as "enemies of the human race, rather than of human error" (*Apol.* 37, ANF 3.45). Common opinion treated Christians as scapegoats responsible for floods and droughts, pestilence, and famine. It is this aspect of the matter that drives Tertullian beyond the paradox of alien citizenship. Though he begins by recognizing that Christians are both involved in and disengaged from society, he ends by welcoming the charge that Christians are enemies of pagan society and by insisting that they break all ties with a world totally corrupted by idolatry.

---

[5] See also Tertullian, *Apol.* 37 (ANF 3.45): ". . . almost all the inhabitants of your various cities being followers of Christ."

Tertullian's project, then, is consciously like Noah's. His city, indeed his entire world, is doomed. The doom is evident in the pervasive presence of idolatry. The Christian encounters idols not merely in the temples but in the baths, the marketplace, the theater, the circus, the arena, and in private as well as public associations. The problem is not so much how to find a place to stand in Roman society, as how to escape involvement in it. The urban life of late antiquity effectively removed privacy as an option. No one could easily escape being a part of the urban life around him. For Tertullian's Christian, life was a desperate attempt to escape the pollution and filth surrounding him on all sides. Christians were to avoid not only the temples but all public amusements. They might not be idol makers or astrologers, panders or gladiators. Idolatry with its attendant immorality so corrupted other professions that Christians were forbidden to become teachers, soldiers, or civil servants (*On Idolatry* 7–11; 17, ANF 3.64ff; 71f.).[6] The ark of the church alone provided a refuge, and even there the Christian ran the risk of being washed overboard before gaining access to the majestic spectacle of the universal deluge. Only the pure might board the ark.

Like his attitude toward society, Tertullian's attitude toward philosophy illustrates initial acceptance but final rejection of the marvelous paradox of alien citizenship. The paradox cannot finally be maintained. Tertullian begins by accepting Justin Martyr's solution to the problem of the relation between Christian and pagan truth. From one point of view there is continuity. Both by reading the Old Testament and by using their natural reason, the Greek philosophers caught glimpses of the truth. The soul is naturally Christian, and its kingship with the Word of God enables it to find truth. From another point of view, however, there is discontinuity. What the philosophers saw dimly and partially has now been revealed in Christ clearly and fully. Truth is the same wherever it may be found, and all truth is Christ's. But it is only in the incarnate Word that we find truth complete and available to all. Tertullian begins with Justin's paradox of continuity and discontinuity, but he ends by moving beyond the paradox and rejecting philosophy altogether. The philosophers disagree with one another because each treats his partial glimpse of the truth as the whole and draws mistaken conclusions. They therefore teach immorality. Socrates was possessed by a demon. One can only conclude that Athens has nothing to do with Jerusalem.

It is Tertullian's attitude towards martyrdom that more than anything else demonstrates how he fails to maintain the marvelous paradox. The martyr in prison has in reality been delivered from the prison house of the world (*Ad Martyras* 2, ANF 3. 693f.). Like the desert for the prophet, prison enables the martyr to exhibit fully his alien character. In principle, the Christian has never been part of the city in which he lives. Martyrdom

---

[6] See also Hippolytus, *The Apostolic Tradition*, ed. Gregory Dix (reissued with corrections, preface and bibliography by Henry Chadwick. London: SPCK, 1968), p. 24ff.

completes the severing of ties to that city. Tertullian may have edited the *Martyrdom of Perpetua and Felicitas.* Even if he did not, he would have agreed with its understanding of martydom. For Perpetua, prison is a palace. Embracing it involves a total and cruel rejection of her father, family, and city. This attitude, which contradicts the marvelous paradox of the letter to Diognetus, was widespread in early Christianity. Eusebius tells of five Christians martyred in the Diocletian persecution in Egypt. When the governor asks them who they are, they give the names of prophets. And when asked their city,

> [The spokesman] answered that Jerusalem was his country. . . . But [Firmilian] inquiring closely and curiously what this might be, and where it lay, was answered, "It was a city to be the homeland only of the righteous, for none but those should have a share in it; and it lay toward the east, toward the rising sun."[7]

For Tertullian, as for many other early Christians, the paradox fails. The alien character of Christianity dominates. The only city that matters is the heavenly Jerusalem.

Clement of Alexandria, a contemporary of Tertullian's, in some respects echoes the Latin writer's insistence that Christians are strangers and sojourners, who inhabit cities but despise "the things in the city which are admired by others" and live "in the city as in a desert" (*Stromata* 7.12, ANF 2.545). The Christian's city is heaven, not Athens, Argos, or Sparta; and his lawgiver is God, not Solon, Phoroneus, or Lycurgus. Clement, however, transforms the theme into an approximation of the marvelous paradox:

> But I shall pray the Spirit of Christ to wing me to my Jerusalem. For the Stoics say that heaven is properly a city, but places here on earth are not cities; for they are called so, but are not. For a city is an important thing, and the people a decorous body, and a multitude of men regulated by law as the church by the word—a city on earth impregnable— free from tyranny; a product of the divine will on earth as in heaven. (*Strom.* 4.26, ANF 2.441)

Christians are still thought citizens of the heavenly Jerusalem; but for Clement their citizenship on earth, though alien, is a true citizenship. The heavenly life, freed from tyranny, can in some sense be lived on earth. Moreover, this alien citizenship fulfills the dreams of the Greeks. The Stoics, the poets, and Plato should be able to see in the church the commonwealth for which they yearned. Like Tertullian, Clement thinks of this novel citizenship as a deliverance. But unlike Tertullian, he treats it as a deliverance not merely from but for the world. Heavenly citizenship requires not the dissolution of social ties but their transformation.

---

[7] Eusebius, *Martyrs of Palestine* 11.7–19. Cited by Ramsay MacMullen in *Enemies of the Roman Order* (Cambridge: Harvard University Press, 1966), p. 91.

Clement's understanding of idolatry is crucial to his espousal of the paradox. Humanity once possessed "the truly noble freedom of those who lived as free citizens under heaven" (*Exhortation to the Heathen* 1, ANF 2.172). But idolatry placed its yoke on the entire created order and turned humanity "from the heavenly life, and stretched [it] on the earth, by inducing [it] to cleave to earthly objects" (*Ex. Heath.* 2, ANF 2.178). Idolatry in its many different manifestations is "the fountain of insensate wickedness" (*Ex. Heath.* 3, ANF 2.184). Failing to know the good involves failing to do the good, and so idolatry explains the human predicament.

In these opinions Clement is simply giving expression to themes that are commonplace not only in early Christian writings but also in Judaism. But he goes one step further, by associating idolatry with custom. The ancestral customs of the gentiles are idolatrous chains that bind humanity in superstition, ignorance of the truth, and licentiousness. Custom, then, must be avoided like the island of the sirens:

> Sail past the song: it works death. Exert your will only, and you have overcome ruin; bound to the wood of the cross, thou shalt be free from destruction: the Word of God will be thy pilot, and the Holy Spirit will bring thee to anchor in the haven of heaven. (*Ex. Heath.* 12, ANF 2.205)

Like Ulysses bound to the mast, Christians are freed from the lethal effects of the old songs of custom and idolatry and able to join in the harmony of the new song, the harmony that first ordered creation and now brings the order of redemption.

Two further themes distinguish Clement's attitude from Tertullian's. Like Tertullian he insists that Christians must be aliens by breaking their connection with idolatry and with their ancestral customs. But Clement makes this appeal to all humanity, not just to Christians. Moreover, breaking with custom does not mean a break with the world:

> We do not abolish social intercourse, but look with suspicion on the snares of custom, and regard them as a calamity. (*The Instructor* 2.1, ANF 2.239)

In other words, the social ties of late antiquity are condemned only to the degree that they are tainted with idolatry. Once freed from that bondage, they can be used and transformed. The detailed teaching of *The Instructor* and the point of view of the discourse titled "Who is the Rich Man that is Saved?" both focus on this theme. All things can be rescued from bondage and transformed to their proper value by being made God's. The marvelous paradox is asserted by the Christian Platonists of Alexandria: a Christian becomes a citizen as well as an alien. Clement would agree with Origen that,

> Christians do more good to their countries than the rest of mankind, since they educate the citizens and teach them to be devoted to God,

the guardian of their city; and they take those who have lived good lives in the most insignificant cities up to a divine and heavenly city.[8]

Clement's attitude toward Greek philosophy seems designed to maintain the same paradox, though it may be that it runs the risk of losing the paradox in too positive an assessment of philosophical truth. Like Tertullian he follows the schema we first encounter in Justin Martyr. The philosophers derived their truth either from the Old Testament or from "certain scintillations of the divine Word" in their minds (*Ex. Heath.* 5–7, ANF 2.190ff). This means that they spoke truth. Discontinuity, however, is attached to the derivative and partial character of philosophical truth. Like Prometheus the philosophers have stolen "a slender spark, capable of being fanned into flame" (*Strom.* 1.18, ANF 2.320). Like the Bacchae who tore Pentheus asunder, however, they have divided the body of truth. Therefore the multitude fears philosophy as children are terrified of masks. But the fear is unnecessary, because Christianity fans the slender spark to a blaze and unites again the torn body of truth. Moreover, Clement agrees with Philo that philosophy is the handmaid of right religion. It was a pedagogue to the Greeks as the Law was a pedagogue to the Jews. Philosophy continues to provide tools for the defense of the Christian faith. Jerusalem is not to be contrasted with Athens. Instead, "because of the Word the whole world has now become Athens and Greece" (*Ex. Heath.* 11, ANF 2.203). Clement's attitude is the warrant for Christian Platonism and the basis for his attempts to articulate the Gospel in the lingua franca of his day. As with any re-mythologizing, the risk is that the alien character of Christian truth will be lost.

Clement, too, softens the alien character of martyrdom. Its perfection is not so much the completion of a Christian's alienation from society as the exhibition of "the perfect work of love" (*Strom.* 4.4, ANF 2.411). From one point of view martyrdom becomes a metaphor for the Christian life. Its obedience springs neither from fear of punishment nor hope of reward, but from love. And the shedding of faith as spiritual blood is more important than the mere shedding of blood. Christians are not to seek outward martyrdom for its own sake and so "give themselves up to a vain death, as the Gymnosophists of the Indians to useless fire" (*Strom.* 4.4, ANF 2.412). Inner martyrdom is required, a governing of the passions so that the impassibility which makes us as much like God as possible is gained. Clement does not go so far as to agree with the Gnostics that outward martyrdom is to be rejected:

> Those who witness in their life by deed, and at the tribunal by word, whether entertaining hope or surmising fear, are better than those who confess salvation by their mouth alone. But if one ascend also to love, he is a really blessed and true martyr. (*Strom.* 4.9, ANF 2.422)

[8] Origen, *Contra Celsum*, trans. and ed. Henry Chadwick (Cambridge: Cambridge University Press, 1953), p. 509f.

Clement values martyrdom, but only if it is the authentic expression of a Christian life. One should not avoid martyrdom if it comes, but neither should one seek it out, since doing so makes one an active "accomplice in the crime of the persecutor" (*Strom.* 4.10, *ANF* 2.423). A via media between fanaticism and Gnosticism is established, and martyrdom becomes not so much the final alienation of the Christian as the completed expression of a citizenship of love.

Both Tertullian and Clement in their attitudes toward society, Greek philosophy, and martyrdom begin by recognizing the marvelous paradox of alien citizenship. At the same time, both have a tendency to let the paradox dissolve. Tertullian dissolves it by insisting on the alien character of Christianity. In both practice and principle the Christian life dissociates people from social ties. Athens is rejected for the heavenly Jerusalem, and the martyr becomes a sign of perfected alienation from the prison house of the world. In contrast, Clement dissolves the paradox by declaring deliverance not only from the world but for it. Released from bondage to custom and idolatry, society is free to be transfigured. The whole world becomes a better Athens, because it receives the whole of the truth now available to all. The martyr, though in one sense rejecting society, at a deeper level expresses perfect love. Deliverance becomes a reordering of the earthly commonwealth. Thus Clement sets the stage for imperial Christianity of the fourth century.

II. The Imperial Church

The victory of Constantine at the Milvian Bridge in 312, together with his consequent partronage of the Church, must be regarded as a revolution. Like all revolutions, however, it was in one sense the product of complicated forces already at work in society, and held unforeseen implications for the future.

It is difficult enough to understand Constantine's conversion; it is virtually impossible to describe accurately its relation to Christianity as a social phenomenon in the ancient world. It seems most reasonable to understand Constantine's conversion as his gradual commitment to the church, culminating in his deathbed baptism. Presumably he began by understanding Christ as another manifestation of *Sol Invictus*, for the imperial patronage of Christianity did not immediately mean the suppression of paganism. Indeed, Christianity can scarcely be regarded as the official religion of the empire until Theodosius the Great's edict of 380, promulgating the emperor's wish that all his subjects be Christian. Moreover, Constantine's motives in espousing Christianity were related to the accepted idea of the *pax deorum*. To appease the God of the Christians was to gain his power in ordering the Roman world. That Constantine could be convinced of this idea, must in some way have been related to his recognition of Christianity's power in human lives. At any rate, in the emperor's decision we seem to be dealing with one case of what Peter Brown calls "spontaneous combustion arising from friction within a system of widely shared ideas."[9]

The sort of vision we have found in Clement, of a divine deliverance capable of reordering society, erupted in a variety of contexts in the third and early fourth centuries. It was a vision capable of supplying an ideology for Constantine's political and religious settlement. To the degree that it became an ideology for Rome, the vision of alien citizenship lost its paradoxical character, and the danger implicit in Clement's position became explicit. We find two examples of that ideology in Eusebius of Caesarea's *Panegyric of Constantine* and in Lactantius's *Divine Institutes*.

Shortly before Constantine's death, Eusebius delivered a panegyric in celebration of the thirtieth anniversary of the emperor's accession. His theme was "one God, one empire":

> When that instrument of our redemption, the thrice holy body of Christ was raised, the energy of these evil spirits was at once destroyed. . . and one God was proclaimed to all mankind. At the same time one universal power, the Roman empire, arose and flourished, while the enduring and implacable hatred of nation against nation was now removed. (*Panegyric* 16, NPNF 2.1.606)

It should be noted that the ideal is no longer the city but the universal commonwealth, which Eusebius identifies with the empire. Clement's vision of a transfigured social order is identified here with the political order, and Christians consequently lose their alien character.

Eusebius's description is exaggerated; but it is not merely rhetorical. He compares the present to the past:

> Peace, the happy nurse of youth, extended her reign throughout the world. Wars were no more, for the gods were not: no more did warfare in country or town, no more did the effusion of human blood, distress mankind, as heretofore, when demon-worship and the madness of idolatry prevailed. (*Pan.* 8, NPNF 2.1.592)

Civil war had indeed been replaced by peace and order; Eusebius's verdict, while exaggerated, clearly had a basis in fact. What is more important, however, is his explanation of the restored Pax Romana. The suppression of polytheism and idolatry has restored order. Warfare was the legacy of the pagan city. By proclaiming one God, all cities could be united under a single commonwealth. Thus Constantinian order had a spiritual as well as a political dimension. Victory over the barbarians corresponded with triumph over the spiritual barbarians, the demons, whom pagans worshipped as their gods. Imperial sponsorship of church building projects, together with the plunder-

---

[9] Peter Brown, *The Making of Late Antiquity* (Cambridge: Harvard University Press, 1978), p. 7.

ing of pagan temples, were outward signs of this spiritual victory. Constantine was seen as God's vice-regent in securing for the world this sacralized order.

One kind of language in which Eusebius explains this new order is drawn from the solar religion employed earlier by Elagabalus and Aurelian, as well as by Constantine. Eusebius begins his oration by cleverly protecting this pagan language from misunderstanding. The celebration is in honor of "the Great Sovereign himself," and it becomes clear that this King is God, to whom the emperor addresses his praises, and whom "the all-radiant sun" obeys. The panegyric continues by describing God's providential governance of the whole created order, a governance administered by "His only begotten preexistent Word, the great High Priest of the mighty God." The Word is called

> that Light, which transcendent above the universe, encircles the Father's Person, interposing and dividing between the eternal, uncreated Essence and all derived existence: that Light which, streaming from on high, proceeds from that Deity who knows not origin or end, and illumines the super-celestial regions, and all that heaven itself contains, with the radiance of wisdom bright beyond the splendor of the sun. (*Pan.* 1, *NPNF* 2.1.583)

This rich (and Origenist, if not Arianizing) description of the Word depicts Him as the true *Sol Invictus*. Constantine is his "friend," his *comes*, acting as interpreter to the Word of God (*Pan.* 2, *NPNF* 2.1.583). As such, the emperor can be described as the sun, resembling "his Divine example." The four Caesars form a *quadriga* (four-horse chariot) whereby Constantine is enabled to illumine the whole of the empire. Invested "with a semblance of heavenly sovereignty," the emperor "frames his earthly government according to the pattern of that Divine original" (*Pan.* 3, *NPNF* 2.1.584).

The hierarchical structure, by which sovereignty is passed from the Father through his Word to Constantine, enables Eusebius to apply solar theology both to the Word and to the emperor. But it is important to note that the structure itself is one that derives from Eusebius's Origenist theology. He can use that theology in an unadulterated form by employing Origen's doctrine of the image of God. The Word is that image, and human beings are created "after" the image of God in virtue of their souls. Specifically, Constantine's "reason he derives from the great Source of all reason" (*Pan.* 5, *NPNF* II.1,585). The peculiarity of Eusebius's argument is that Constantine is presented as the perfect human example:

> a Victor in truth, who has gained the victory over those passions which overmaster the rest of men: whose character is formed after the Divine original of the Supreme Sovereign, and whose mind reflects, as in a mirror, the radiance of his virtue. (*Pan.* 5, *NPNF* 2.1.586)

Constantine, then, is the paradigmatic example of a human being created after the image of God and, consequently, the perfect moral exemplar on the human level. The perfect sovereignty he exercises over himself enables him to exercise sovereignty also over everyone else. By weaving together these complicated and eclectic themes into an ideology for the Christian empire, Eusebius succeeds in defining the emperor as the figure who binds the heavenly to the earthly city, thereby effecting a sacralized ordering of the whole world. The risk associated with this view is obvious. The alien character of Christian citizenship is for all practical purposes abolished, so that it becomes possible to reduce the kingdom of God to the kingdom of this world.

Lactantius, the tutor Constantine employed for his family, presents us in the *Divine Institutes* with a platform for the Christian empire not unlike that of Eusebius. To be sure, his treatise is in Latin, not Greek, and it depends far more on Cicero and Stoicism than on Plato for its theoretical structure. Nevertheless, like Eusebius he insists upon the combination of right worship of the one God with the establishment of universal peace and justice. These notions he finds in Cicero's *Republic:*

> The same law, everlasting and unchangeable, will bind all nations at all times; and there will be one common Master and Ruler of all, even God, the framer, arbitrator, and proposer of this law.[10]

This ideal will put an end to the war of city against city. The commonwealth to be established will be based upon a union of religion and wisdom, piety and equity.

In a sense, Lactantius describes the Constantinian empire not only as the realization of the Ciceronian ideal, but also as the restoration of the original order of creation. The reign of Saturn was characterized by recognition of a single God and of his providence. Right religion enables human beings to seek "all things in common" (5.5, ANF 7.140). Once the worship of the one God was taken away, however, and idolatry substituted for it, immorality abounded. More particularly,

> the common intercourse of life perished from among men, and the bond of human society was destroyed. (5.5, ANF 7.141)

With the loss of the knowledge of God, wisdom became separated from religion. The state of human affairs prior to the Christian revelation, then, is described as one of fragmentation in which the vertical bond of humanity to God is broken, with the consequence that the horizontal bond of human beings to one another is shattered as well. Lactantius implies that the function of the Christian state is to restore the age of Saturn.

---

[10] Lactantius, *Div. Inst.* 6.8 (*ANF* 7.171), citing Cicero, *The Republic* 3.22.16. Further references to the *Divine Institutes* are cited with chapter and verse, omitting the title.

In Book 5 of the *Divine Institutes* Lactantius speaks of this restoration under the rubric of justice. Following his classical sources, particularly Cicero, he regards justice as uniting all the virtues, so that it amounts to the chief good for humanity. His analysis focuses upon "piety and equity" as the focal aspects of justice. The former orders human relationship to God; the latter, to one another. Christianity enables the Ciceronian dream to come true, because it alone teaches true piety. And by regarding all human beings as spiritually equal, it teaches true equity for the first time. Justice, understood in this fashion, is the perfect union of religion and wisdom. In Book 7 Lactantius goes on to speak of the Christian hope of the resurrection and of the millennium when "the sacred city shall be planted in the middle of the earth, in which God Himself the builder may dwell together with the righteous" (7.24, ANF 7.219). But he does not long for this millennium. Instead he implores the preservation of Rome, the city that "sustains all things" and restrains the end of the world (7.25, ANF 7.220). Christian eschatology merely decorates the bare bones of Lactantius's argument, and his conclusion resembles that of Cicero in the *Dream of Scipio:*

> Let us serve God with unwearied service, let us keep our posts and watches, let us boldly engage with the enemy whom we know, that victorious and triumphant over our conquered adversary, we may obtain from the Lord that reward of valour which He Himself has promised. (7.27, ANF 7.223)

Emphasis is therefore placed on the sacralized order of the empire rather than its eschatological fulfilment.

To catch a glimpse of how some Christians sought to put the ideology into practice, we must turn to the homilies of John Chrysostom. In one sense, Chrysostom retains the paradox of alien citizenship. The Christian's city, properly speaking, is the heavenly Jerusalem:

> Seeing we are by nature sojourners, let us also be so by choice; that we be not there sojourners and dishonoured, and cast out. For if we are set upon being citizens here, we shall be so neither here nor there; but if we continue to be sojourners, and live in such wise as sojourners ought to live in, we shall enjoy the freedom of citizens both here and there. (*Homily* 16: 2 *Cor.,* NPNF 1.12.359)

It is the conclusion of Chrysostom's exhortation that begins to take us beyond the paradox. The real point of what he says is that our earthly citizenship ought to be so informed by our heavenly that it is transfigured, contributing to the sacralized order of the Christian empire. He makes the point repeatedly. In his introductory homily on Saint Matthew's Gospel he dismisses Plato's "ridiculous republic" and argues that the apostles teach us of the true republic of God. Since that city is no dream, but a heavenly reality, we can participate in it during this life and so find "wealth and poverty, freedom and slavery, life and death, our world and our polity, all changed" (*Hom. 1: Matt.,* NPNF 1.10.5). And in explaining Christ's claim, "My Kingdom is not of this world" (John 18.36), he says Christ makes the denial "not because He doth not rule here, but because He hath His empire from above, and because it is not human, but far greater than this and more splendid" (*Hom. 83: John, NPNF* 1.14.311).

The transfigured citizenship of which Chrysostom speaks depends upon Christ, but its effect is to bind humanity together in a harmony that goes far to characterize both our redemption and God's intention in creation. In his homily on 1 Corinthians 13 Chrysostom weaves together the themes of love, the unity of the human race in Adam, the family, and the city. He employs the Stoic theme (*oikeiosis*), to the effect that the individual appropriates to his love of self the love of family, nation, and universe. These natural forces are "pledges of concord" implanted by God in us (*Hom. 34: 1 Cor., NPNF* 1.12.204).[11] The love for one another that God has created in us explains the institutions of the family and the city. And, by implication, it is the universal commonwealth of Christ that brings God's intention in creation to its perfection.

There is a tension in Chrysostom's understanding of this universal commonwealth. On the one hand, all those who are citizens of the heavenly Jerusalem are equal. Christ exhorts all to come to Him (Matt. 11.28f.) in baptism; there are no longer differences between slave and free, rich and poor.[12] On the other hand, this spiritual and sacramental equality by no means abolishes the hierarchical ordering of society, where, however transformed, these differences remain. Nevertheless, the impact of the spiritual ideal may be found in the realization that the different orders of society need one another and should offer mutual support. The rulers in cities are obliged in principle to ensure this sort of harmony by protecting the weak from the strong (*Hom. 23: Rom., NPNF* 1.11.513). All Christians who are able are repeatedly exhorted to give alms and to care for the poor. At one level, this enterprise is undertaken by the church in its hospitals and hostels. The importance of this public work cannot be exaggerated. We know that Basil the Great's hostel outside Cappadocian Caesarea acted as a magnet for the establishment of a new quarter of the city.[13] Julian the Apostate, in his short-lived attempt to establish an imperial paganism, saw the necessity of founding pagan hostels that would rival the Christian ones and would, like them, assist people regardless of their religious commitments.[14] Chrysostom, of course, approves of this work. But he preaches against treating it as a substitute for private almsgiving and care of the poor and strangers. His

---

[11] See also Chrysostom, *Hom. 19: John, NPNF* 1.14.67: "In this it is that we differ from beasts, for this we have built cities, and markets, and houses, that we may be united one with another, not in the place of our dwelling only, but by the bond of love."

[12] Jean Chrysostom, *Huit Catéchèses Baptismales*, trans. and ed. Antoine Wenger, Sources Chrétiennes 50 (Paris: Les Editions du Cerf, 1957), p. 122.

[13] Gregory Nazianzen, *Panegyric on Saint Basil* 63 (*NPNF* 2.7.416).

[14] Emperior Julian, *Oeuvres Complètes* 1.2, *Lettres*, ed. and trans. Joseph Bidez (Paris: Société d'Edition "Les Belles Lettres," 1960), p. 145.

polemic against ill-used wealth and his exhortations to give alms are a striking feature of his homilies. These works of mercy are the highest form of asceticism, better than virginity itself. Despite discouragement regarding popular response to his preaching, Chrysostom clearly believes that caring for the poor and outcast manifests the universal commonwealth of Christ and the transformed citizenship of this world.

The new citizenship of which Chrysostom speaks is informed also by an ascetical and moral perfection that may be seen most clearly in monasticism. Particularly in the homilies on Matthew, the monks outside Antioch are held up as models of Christian citizenship. Their monasteries are "the city of virtue" (*Hom. 72: Matt., NPNF* 1.10.438). As Athanasius says of Antony, "the desert was made a city by monks, who left their own people and registered themselves for the citizenship in the heavens."[15] Shifting the metaphor slightly, Chrysostom regards the monks as "shining lamps. . . in every part of the earth. . . walls. . . set about the cities" (*Hom. 72: Matt., NPNF* 1.10.439). The monastic life is understood not to be a special form of existence, but the actualization of heavenly citizenship on earth. The Antiochenes are urged to visit the monks and bring their life back to the city:

> For even one dwelling in a city may imitate the self-denial of the monks; yea, one who has a wife, and is busied in a household, may pray, and fast, and learn compunction. . . . The self-denial that is practised in the deserts, let us bring into our cities. (*Hom. 55: Matt., NPNF* 1.10.344)

What Chrysostom means by this is made clear by his detailed exhortations concerning the theater, the baths, family and social duties, and economic obligations. He envisions an urban life purified and transformed by the monastic ideal.

The theme engages his attention to such a degree that he can even regard the monks as second-rate Christians because they have not tested their ideal in the turbulent waters of urban life. They affirm the ideal, but its full value is realized only when put into practice in difficult circumstances. For this reason, Chrysostom, ordinarily an admirer of monasticism, goes so far as to attack the monks:

> They, who were living virtuously, and who under any circumstances might have confidence, have taken possession of the tops of the mountains, and have escaped out of the world, just as if they were tearing themselves from an enemy and an alien, instead of from a body to which they belonged. (*Hom. 6: Eph.*)[16]

---

[15] Athanasius, *Life of Antony* 14, *Athanasius: The Life of Antony and the Letter to Marcellinus*, trans. and intro. Robert C. Gregg, Classics of Western Spirituality (New York: The Paulist Press, 1980), p.42f.

[16] The translation is that of the *Library of the Fathers of the Holy Catholic Church (LF)* (Oxford: John Henry Parker, 1845), p.165. The *NPNF* translation interprets the passage slightly differently, in such a way as to reverse its meaning: ". . . and have escaped out of the world, separating themselves as from an enemy and an alien and not from a body to

The movement should be in the opposite direction. Though one can learn to steer the ship of his life in the quiet harbor of the monastery, the true test comes when the ship enters the stormy seas of the earthly city (*Hom*. 21: *Eph.*, *NPNF* 1.13.155). The ambivalence in Chrysostom's attitude toward monasticism is easily explained. He is committed to the ideal as the Christian ideal, but he is concerned that its transforming power not be lost.

The most difficult question to answer is what result was achieved by Christians like Eusebius, Lactantius, and Chrysostom. Of course, the empire had become Christian; and this meant that the Christian church became a central, powerful, and wealthy institution in late antiquity. It is possible to argue that the church served the cause of *Romanitas*, breathing new life into the old forms. It is more difficult to argue that ordinary citizenship was transformed in an obvious or far-reaching way. A. H. M. Jones, examining the question, concludes that "the general standards of conduct. . . remained in general static and in some respects . . . sunk.""[17] The closest he can come to an explanation of this astonishing conclusion is that the Christians set their ideal so high that it could not be realized and was, consequently, not attempted by most. It is difficult to disagree. Perhaps, however, the conclusion could be elaborated by suggesting that the ideal itself had become corrupted by losing touch with the paradox of alien citizenship. The ideal became a transformed citizenship and so implied that heaven had been or could be brought to earth. The message of deliverance yielded to a message of reordering. And what tended to happen was that heaven was reduced to earth rather than earth drawn toward heaven.

The alien character of Christian citizenship is affirmed by preachers like Chrysostom, but it ceases to be an essential part of the message. There are, to be sure, some counterweights. The monasticism of the post-Constantinian period, for example, looks like a protest against a church gone public and an attempt to retain the spirit of the martyrs. But as a protest movement, it was soon co-opted by the church. The work of Athanasius, the Cappadocians, and even Chrysostom tamed monasticism and limited its ability to witness to the alien character of Christian citizenship. Ecclesiastical resistance to imperial control of the church, as well as to the heretical emperors, can also be regarded as a counterweight; and the tightening of catechetical requirements might also be added to the list. But none of these counterweights sufficed to maintain the paradox of alien citizenship.

III. Conclusion: The Importance of the Paradox

It is tempting to conclude that, however viable as an ideal, alien citizenship cannot be put into practice on a social scale. Tertullian felt obliged to insist upon the alien character of Christianity, but his program

[17] Arnold H. M. Jones, *The Later Roman Empire* (Norman, Okla.: University of Oklahoma Press, 1964), 2: 979.

could not be implemented save by martydom, because only martydom could sever the social ties linking the Christian to the earthly society. Clement tended to emphasize the other side of the paradox, but this ran the risk of losing the message of deliverance in that of a new order. And the Christian empire, by claiming to realize his dream, succeeded only in creating a new social order that was more earthly than heavenly. On the other hand, perhaps a dialectic is at work. Indeed, the very impossibility of realizing the paradox may be its genuine value. Let me briefly examine a theme in Augustine's thought as a way of elaborating this suggestion.

Without entering into any full discussion of Augustine, the central point can nonetheless be made that he restates the marvelous paradox of alien citizenship originally advanced in the letter to Diognetus. In the *City of God*, written a few years before his death in 430, Augustine raises the question of the chief good for human beings.[18] That chief good is to be regarded as social, and understood as the perfect union of peace and everlasting life (19.11). The concluding section of the nineteenth book (21–28) is a considered discussion of Scipio's definition of a commonwealth in Cicero's *Republic* and an attempt to show how peace is and is not a characteristic of human society in this life. Scipio defines the commonwealth as "the weal of the people." By "people" he means a multitude "united in association by a common sense of right and a community of interest (21). Crucial to this understanding is the notion of justice. Augustine (like Lactantius) understands justice to involve worship of the true God and his rule over "an obedient City":

> In consequence the soul rules the body in all men who belong to this City and obey God, and the reason faithfully rules the vices in a lawful system of subordination; so that just as the individual righteous man lives on the basis of faith which is active in love, so the association, or people, of righteous men lives on the same basis of faith, active in love, the love with which a man loves God as God ought to be loved, and loves his neighbour as himself. (23)

Augustine, however, refuses to conclude that the Christian empire fits this definition of a commonwealth. Only the city of God, the future destination of the pilgrim saints, will fulfill the ideal. Augustine begins by insisting upon the alien character of the Christian city, but he argues that the two cities are mixed in this life. This conclusion means that the empire can in one sense foreshadow the city of God. The people of God can "make use of the peace of Babylon" (26). They are citizens on earth as well as aliens. The paradox is that the Christian saint possesses the peace of the city of God in a double fashion; in this life, "by faith," in the world to come, "by open vision" eternally (27). The paradox really describes an attitude toward the Christian

---

[18] Augustine, *City of God* 19.21, ed. David Knowles (Harmondsworth, Middlesex, England: Penguin Books, 1972), p. 881ff. Further references are to this edition.

life. This life with its associations and duties must be taken seriously. Thus in one way Augustine gives a primacy to the world of our experience. We must be citizens. Nevertheless, our experience is that of a pilgrim or a convalescent; it takes on its true meaning only when related to our destiny in the city of God. And so we are aliens.

Augustine's statement of the paradox makes a certain amount of sense. What is less clear is its meaning in practice. Indeed, in the fifth century we can begin to see the same polarities found in Tertullian and Clement. The sack of Rome by Alaric in 410 was not only the occasion for Augustine's *City of God;* it also sent shock waves throughout the whole empire. Jerome in Bethlehem asked what was safe if Rome perished. It became increasingly clear during the fifth century that the order of Christian Rome had collapsed in the West. Deliverance once again became the theme of Christian writers. Salvian of Marseilles looked at his world toward the middle of the fifth century and raised the anguished question why God should allow His people to suffer and to be conquered by barbarians. He gives as his answer: "[God] suffers us to endure these trials because we deserve to endure them."[19] This judgment is supported by a detailed indictment of Roman Christian society. The moral Salvian draws is that we must be Christian in deed as well as word, and his model is an ascetical one. The servants of God show us what we must do. Repentance, withdrawal from the evils of society, and growth in holiness alone hold up the hope of deliverance. Salvian's program is not unlike Tertullian's. And it does seem that in the early Middle Ages the monasteries supplied the arks in which many Christians sought to live through the cataclysm of the West's collapse.

Clearly, however, Salvian's was not the only point of view. Rutilius Namatianus, returning in 416 to a Gaul devastated by the Visigoths, sees the situation as a challenge to rebuild. His loyalty is to Rome: "What was only a world you have made a city."[20] And the city must be rebuilt. He shudders upon seeing monks; whether mad, evil, or ill, they are to be condemned for abandoning the human world. Namatianus was probably not a Christian, but there were many Christians who agreed with him. Like Clement of Alexandria, they looked for deliverance not merely from the horrors of their day, but for their society. One need only think of Apollinaris Sidonius and his work. It was Christians like these that used the church, and particularly the monasteries, as a means for restoring order to society. The monastery supplied deliverance from the world, but it also became an ordering principle in building medieval Europe.

The conclusion I wish to draw is that the paradox of alien citizenship can

---

[19] Salvian, *On the Government of God* 4.12, trans. Eva M. Sanford (New York: Columbia University Press, 1930), p. 119.

[20] Rutilius Claudius Namatianus, *Concerning his Return,* in *The Last Poets of Imperial Rome,* trans. Harold Isbell (Harmondsworth, Middlesex, England: Penguin Books, 1971), p. 222.

never be successfully put into practice on a social scale. All the figures I have discussed state the paradox as an ideal; but in trying to actualize it, they break it. In a context where the Christian message was understood as one of deliverance from society, there were those like Tertullian who ended by seeing only the alien character of the Christian life. But there were also those like Clement, who saw deliverance as a gift to the world. Inevitably, this attitude ended by changing the message of Christianity from one of deliverance to one of ordering and sanctifying the world. And so the alien character of Christianity was lost. In Augustine's time the collapse of the empire in the West meant that there Christianity was once more obliged to speak its message as one of deliverance from the world. And the pattern repeated itself. Deliverance sometimes meant withdrawal from the human city; often it became a way of reordering it. The revolution of today becomes the establishment of tomorrow and invites a further transformation. The contemplation of the heavenly city works upon the human heart and enables the Christian to be an alien citizen whatever his circumstances, whatever his calling.

5

Worship in Urban Life:
The Example of Medieval Constantinople

JOHN F. BALDOVIN, S. J.
Jesuit School of Theology at Berkeley

> The City of the Mother of God consecrates itself to her as an offering, for she resides in it. Through her the city is both protected and powerful. And so the city cries to her: "Hail, O hope of all the ends of the earth."[1]

The city in question is, of course, Constantinople. This poetic prayer accompanied psalmody at morning prayer (or *orthros*) at Constantinople on the fifth Sunday of Lent, and acted as a refrain to a processional psalm on the anniversary of the city's dedication, 11 May. Such allusions to the protection of Constantinople, the God-guarded city, by the Mother of God are not at all rare in the city's medieval liturgy. In fact, anyone who attempts to reconstruct the tenth- and eleventh-century system of worship at Byzantium cannot help but notice how frequently the city is referred to in liturgical texts, and how much the city itself figures in worship.

I would like to lay out the relationship between the Christian worship and the urban milieu of Constantinople in the Middle Byzantine period, that period for which our sources are particularly rich. I will do this in three parts, showing first, how the history of Constantinople was celebrated throughout its yearly cycle of worship; second, how the city itself, and not merely its churches and shrines, acted as a locus for Christian worship; and finally, how the city was considered to be sanctified by worship.

I. The City in the Liturgical Year

The *Typikon*, a book of directions for the patriarch's liturgical services at Constantinople in the tenth century, provides us with a rather complete

---

[1] Juan Mateos, ed., *Le typicon de la grande église (Ms. HS 40)*, Orientalia Christiana Analecta 165 (Rome: Pont. Institutum Orientalium Studiorum) 1: 286. Abbreviated in text as *Typikon*.

picture of the city's major liturgical services. It shows a number of days that were given over, not to the celebration of a particular facet of Christian faith, such as the Epiphany, the Exaltation of the Holy Cross, or the Ascension, nor to the memory of particular Christian saints, but rather to anniversaries of specific events in the history of Constantinople. By my count there are twenty such commemorations listed in the tenth-century *Typikon*. All but two of these commemorations involved liturgical processions.

By far the most important of these celebrations was the anniversary of the city's dedication, an event that took place on 11 May 330, some four years after Constantine had decided to make the old Byzantium into his capital. To what extent the city's dedication in 330 was specifically Christian is a point of some discussion. It seems most reasonable to follow Gilbert Dagron, who in his masterful history of the city's first hundred years, *Naissance d'une capitale*,[2] claims that Constantinople was not so much dedicated to the Christian God or to pagan deities as it was to the glory of the emperor after whom it was named. Nevertheless, it was not long before the city was thought to have been dedicated to Christ or to the God of the Martyrs.[3] By the seventh century, Mary, the Mother of God, was considered the object of dedication, especially after she was credited with defending the city in the siege of 626. And so in the tenth-century *Typikon* it is the Mother of God who has pride of place in the anniversary of the city's dedication. The title for the day reads: "11 May. The commemoration of the birthday of this God-protected and royal city" (*Typikon* 1.286).

The liturgical celebration began, as do all major feasts in the Byzantine church year, with evening prayer or *paramonie* on the previous evening. This was a solemn affair held in the Great Church (Hagia Sophia) and followed by a monastic vigil service called *pannychis*. The next morning the Great Church was again the locale for the celebration of *orthros*. At both evening prayer and morning prayer the special chant of the day was the one which introduces this essay: "The City of the Mother of God consecrates itself to her.' . . ." Since Mary was responsible for the city's welfare and dominion, Constantinople owed her its allegiance.

After *orthros* a liturgical procession (involving participation of the whole people and not merely officials) moved from the Great Church down the major boulevard of the city, the Mese, to the most important plaza, the Forum of Constantine. It was here, precisely at the porphyry column topped by a statue of Constantine portrayed as a Christianized sun-god, that the original dedicatory service had been held. The small oratory at the base of

---

[2] Gilbert Dagron, *Naissance d'une capitale: Constantinople et ses institutions de 330 à 451* (Paris: Presses universitaires de France, 1974), p. 41.

[3] Eusebius, *Vita Constantini* 3.48. See also D. Lathoud, "La consécration et dédicace de Constantinople d'après la tradition byzantine," *Echos d'Orient* 23 (1924): 289–314 and 24 (1925): 180–201, and Richard Krautheimer, *Three Christian Capitals: Topography and Politics* (Berkeley and Los Angeles: University of California, 1983), pp. 41–68.

the porphyry column, the chapel of Constantine and Helen, was the focus for the anniversary celebration. The place was made even more significant by its legendary associations, for it was said to contain not only nails from the cross of Christ but also the Palladium of old Rome. More than any other place in the city, therefore, this plaza with its column represented the noble ancestry of Constantinople: Constantinian, Christian, and Roman.

The outdoor liturgical celebration of the city's birthday was one of five such yearly services that included special readings before the procession moved elsewhere for the celebration of the Eucharist. The choice of readings at this service illustrates the way the citizens of Constantinople made a connection between their city and their religious faith. The first reading, Acts 18.1–11, contains two verses that the Constantinopolitans would especially apply to themselves (although they had to stretch for references, since Byzantium is not mentioned in the New Testament). The first is Paul's announcement: "From now on I will go to the Gentiles." The second is the word of the Lord in reference to Corinth: "For I have many people in this city." The gospel for the service was also specially chosen for its applicability to Constantinople. One phrase in John's Last Supper discourse, John 15.9–16, reads: "You did not choose me, but I chose you, that you should go out and bear fruit, and that your fruit should abide. . . ." No doubt the Byzantines thought the statement applicable to themselves.

Those accustomed to the concept of civil religion will perhaps smile; for here church, crown, and city are virtually identified with each other. The inhabitants of Constantinople, at least in their prayers, considered themselves to have a very special place in the world and attributed that prominent position to God's continuing providence. Medieval Byzantines believed in general that their *civitas* or civilization was to play a special eschatological role as the remnant of the redeemed. This role is even more evident in the chant used on 11 May for the procession's return to the Great Church:

> O Lord, deliver your city, the eye of the world, from all your just threats; conserve it always as the ornament of the imperial sceptre. Grant us, by the help of the Mother of God, protection from the barbarians and safety from all dangers. (*Typikon* 1, 286)

Of course, the city's birthday was an obvious day on which to relate its history to its established religious faith. But there were nineteen days besides, in which a civic anniversary was celebrated liturgically. Each of these commemorations referred to a time when the city was saved from disaster by God and the Mother of God. These near-catastrophes included fires, barbarian attacks, and earthquakes. Earthquakes, especially, evoked not only immediate liturgical response but lasting memorial observances. They must have been terrifying events, all the more so because they were understood as particular signs of divine displeasure. There are nine such earthquake memorials in the tenth-century *Typikon* of the Great Church.

Most of the services related to these commemorations took place outside the city walls or at the edge of the city, where there was much open space. (The city never grew to the extent of the fifth-century Theodosian Walls.) This choice of liturgical site probably reflects the tendency of the population to flee to open areas in case of earthquake, as we would do today.

Other commemorations referred to the city's salvation from human threats, namely attacks and sieges. Here the Mother of God played an especially active role in the city's defense. One of the most vivid examples is that of the attack of the Avars and Persians in 626, when Heraclius was fighting Persians elsewhere and the army was for the most part absent from the city. On this occasion, according to Byzantine tradition, it was a relic, the robe of the Virgin, kept in a chapel at the shrine of Blachernae near the northernmost point of the city walls, that saved the day. The Patriarch Sergius paraded this new palladium around the city walls, and the enemies fell back in disarray. Thus the chant for the Feast of the Deposition of the Virgin's Robe, on 2 July (a feast still celebrated in Byzantine churches today), reads in the *Typikon:*

> O Mother of God, ever Virgin, protection of all peoples, you have given
> to your city your Robe and Cincture as sure protection. By your virginal
> conception, you remained incorruptible, for in you time and nature
> have entered a new way. And so we beg you: Give peace to our empire,
> and to our souls great mercy. (*Typikon* 1.328)

Earthquakes, barbarian invasions, sieges, fires, and other disasters all provided likely occasions for services of prayer if not panicky supplication. What is so remarkable about the worship system of medieval Constantinople is not that these events were times for immediate liturgical expression, but that their anniversaries were commemorated year after year for centuries. In the West, Rome and Gaul knew supplicatory processions that occurred every year on fixed days, or according to the date of the Feast of the Ascension; but none were so closely tied to specific local memories. The notion of Constantinople as a sacred, God-guarded city was strong enough to shape the Byzantine liturgical year around events in the city's own history. For this reason alone, Constantinople is an extraordinary example of the conjunction of urban life and Christian worship.

II. The City as a Place of Worship

One of the difficulties we moderns have in reconstructing the worship of late ancient and medieval societies is that we take an anachronistic view of their liturgical life. We tend to think of worship services as isolated events, distinct from the ongoing life of the culture. This was not the case in medieval Constantinople.

Not that Constantinople was unique in its employment of the whole city for worship. Every major urban center of late antiquity had an elaborate liturgical system, in which the major liturgical celebration of each feast or fast occurred in a particular church. This pattern may be called episcopal liturgy, because it was presided over by the bishop of the city or his representative. It has also been called stational liturgy, from the Roman idea that each major liturgical assembly was a *statio*, a "standing on guard duty of God's people."[4] Rome, Jerusalem, Antioch, Alexandria, Ravenna, Milan, Mainz, Metz—all of these cities had stational systems of worship in which different churches or shrines in and around the city were employed on different days. For the most part, this would be the city's only liturgical celebration on that day; but the station could also stand for the most important liturgical celebration, while less grand events were held in other churches for the convenience of the faithful. In either case, stational liturgies were major public celebrations that linked Christian worship with the ongoing life of the city, especially by means of processions.

Constantinople also followed this pattern. To be sure, it had a more centralized focus for the celebration of the Eucharist on major feasts. The Great Church, Hagia Sophia, was located at the heart of the city's monumental center, close by the Imperial Palace, the Hippodrome, and the Forum of Constantine. The great feasts of the liturgical year, such as Christmas, Epiphany, the Paschal Vigil, Easter Sunday, the Transfiguration (6 August), and the Exaltation of the Holy Cross (14 September), were all celebrated in the Great Church. Aside from these, however, a great number of feasts were celebrated at different churches in or around the city. These were not minor celebrations, for the tenth-century *Typikon* of the Great Church indicates that they, too, included liturgical processions.

All in all, some sixty-eight processions were held during the year. Moreover, this evidence is corroborated by the *De ceremoniis aulae byzantinae* ("On the Ceremonies of the Byzantine Court") compiled by the tenth-century emperor-scholar, Constantine VII Porphyrogenitus. This source describes among other things the involvement of the imperial court in liturgical processions.[5] The emperor and his retinue participated in twenty-six liturgical processions in the course of the year. Of these, nine were processions from the imperial palace to the Great Church. These short but highly stylized progresses were not really popular processions but rather what I call "personage-centered" processions. On seventeen other occasions the emperor and his court joined with popular liturgical processions that had as their terminus a church other than Hagia Sophia.

In any case, an imperial procession was a splendid affair. One of these is

4 See my two essays, "La liturgie stationnale à Constantinople," *La Maison Dieu* 147 (1981): 85–94 and "The City as Church, the Church as City," *Liturgy: Holy Places* 3:4 (1983): 69–73. See also Geoffrey G. Willis, "Roman Stational Liturgy," in his *Further Essays on Early Roman Liturgy*, Alcuin Club Collections 50 (London: SPCK, 1968), pp. 3–20.

5 Johann Jacob Reiske, ed., *De ceremoniis aulae byzantinae*, Corpus Scriptorum Historiae Byzantinae 8 and 9, 2 vols. (Bonn: Weber, 1829–40).

described by Harun-ibn-Yahya, an Arab captive at the court of Basil I, the Macedonian, in the last quarter of the ninth century. I shall quote here from A. A. Vasiliev's translation:

> The Emperor commands that on his way from the Gate of the Palace to the Church for the common people (the Great Church), which is in the middle of the city, be spread mats and upon them be strewn aromatic plants and green foliage, and that on the right and left of his passage the walls be adorned with brocade. Then he is preceded by 10,000 elders wearing clothes of red brocade; their hair reaches their shoulders, and they wear no upper cloak. Then behind them come 10,000 young men wearing clothes of white brocade. Then come 10,000 servants wearing clothes of brocade of the color of the blue sky; in their hands they hold axes covered with gold. Behind them follow 5,000 chosen eunuchs wearing white Khorasanian clothes of half-silk; in their hands they hold golden crosses. Then after them come 10,000 Turkish and Khorasanian pages wearing striped breast plates; in their hands they hold spears and shields wholly covered with gold. Then come a hundred most dignified patricians wearing clothes of colored brocade; in their hands they have golden censers perfumed with aloes. Then come twelve chief patricians wearing clothes woven with gold; each of them holds a golden rod. Then come a hundred pages wearing clothes trimmed with borders and adorned with pearls; they carry a golden case in which is the Imperial Robe for the Emperor's prayer. Then before the Emperor comes a man called al-Ruhum, who makes the people be silent and says "Be silent." Then comes an old man holding in his hand a golden wash-basin and a golden jug adorned with pearls and rubies. Then comes the Emperor wearing his festival clothes, that is, silk clothes woven with jewels; on his head there is a crown; he wears two shoes, one of them black, the other red. The prime minister follows him. In the hand of the Emperor there is a small golden box in which is a bit of earth. He goes on foot. Whenever he makes two paces, the minister says in their own language "*Memnesthe tou thanatou,*" which means in translation "Remember the death." When the minister says this to him, the Emperor pauses, opens the box, looks at the earth, kisses it, and weeps. He proceeds in this way until he reaches the gate of the Church.[6]

Doubtless, Harun-ibn-Yahya's estimate of over fifty-five thousand participants in the imperial procession from palace to church is grossly exaggerated. But one certainly gets the impression that these processions were extravagant affairs, for the *De ceremoniis* informs us that there were also stopping points along the way in which the leaders of the various traditional urban factions (Blues, Greens, Whites, and Reds) greeted the emperor with acclamations, many of a religious character. These are clear indications that the public worship life of Constantinople linked court, church, and society very closely together.

---

[6] A. A. Vasiliev, "Harum Ibn-Yahya and his Description of Constantinople," *Seminarium Kondokovianum* 5 (1932): 158–60.

Let us return to the *Typikon's* descriptions of the liturgical processions. I have already mentioned that there were sixty-eight popular processions in the course of a year. These processions always had an appropriate church or shrine for their destination. For example, they went to a church dedicated to the Virgin Mary on her feast days; or on 18 October, the feast of Saint Luke, they went to the Church of the Holy Apostles where his relics were deposited. Many of these processions involved travelling considerable distances, since the starting point was usually the Great Church. The *Typikon* indicates that eleven processions went to Holy Apostles (five kilometers from the Great Church), ten to the shrine of the Mother of God at Blachernae (seven kilometers), and three to the Hebdomon, the former army camp outside the city walls on the Via Egnatia to Rome (ten kilometers). These were by no means the only long processions in the course of the liturgical year.

In order to give an idea of what these processions were like, I will follow the *Typikon's* description of what happened on 25 September. The reason given for the procession is "the terrors which announced the resurrection," i.e., an earthquake in 437, when Theodosius II was emperor and Proclus was patriarch (*Typikon* 1.44ff). According to a legend chronicled by Theophanes, it was during the procession of the terrified supplicants on 25 September 437 that the Trisagion was miraculously revealed. Each year on this anniversary the patriarch, clergy, and people would assemble in the Great Church after morning prayer (which ended around dawn) and go in procession to the Forum of Constantine, where they would stop for a brief service of prayer and litanies. They would then proceed down the Mese to the Golden Gate, where they would stop again briefly. They then processed, singing all the while, to the open-air Tribunal of the Hebdomon, where a number of emperors were crowned or acclaimed by the army. The chant for the procession was, of course, the Trisagion, which had been revealed on this day. After the procession came to a halt there was a service of psalms, scripture readings, and litanies. Finally, the procession moved to the Church of Saint John the Theologian (the Apostle), where the Eucharist was celebrated. The procession and the revelation of the Trisagion are pictured together in the Menologion of Basil II, a product of the eleventh century.[7]

Notice the elements of the liturgical procession: participation of both clergy and people, litanies, the use of open-air spaces for services, and the constant employment of an easily repeatable chant. Especially the use of the city's boulevards and open-air plazas alert us to the public nature of medieval Constantinopolitan worship. Such processions through the streets may have been even more frequent in the pre-Iconoclast period than the *Typikon* indicates. This at least is my suspicion, because Greek church historians of

[7] *Il Menologio de Basilio II (Cod. Vat. gr. 1613)* (Turin: 1907): 2: 65, 142, 350, 353, 355.

the mid-fifth century, namely Socrates and Sozomen, both refer to religious processional practice in Constantinople. The account of Sozomen speaks for itself:

> The Arians, deprived of their churches in Constantinople during the reign of Theodosius (the Great), held their liturgical meetings outside of the city walls. They previously assembled by night in the public porticoes, and were divided into bands, so that they sang antiphonally, for they had composed certain refrains which reflected their own doctrine. At the break of day they marched in procession, singing these hymns, to their liturgical assemblies. They proceeded in this manner on all solemn festivals and on Sundays and Saturdays. . . . John (Chrysostom) was fearful that any of his own people be led astray by witnessing these processions, and therefore commanded them to sing hymns in the same manner. The orthodox became more distinguished, in a brief time surpassing the heretics in number and processions.[8]

Here we may well have a witness to the origins of liturgical processions in Constantinople. Their frequency in this account (all Sundays, Saturdays, and festivals) has led me to suspect that popular processions were much more frequent in Constantinople in the pre-Iconoclast period than in the ninth and tenth centuries. Moreover, this witness confirms the contention of Juan Mateos and Robert Taft that the introductory rites of the Byzantine Eucharist were influenced directly by Constantinople's stational processions.[9] In addition to frequency of occurrence and effect on the structure of the eucharistic celebration, these processions also show that Christian worship was not confined to the churches, shrines, and monasteries of Constantinople, but that it was an open, public affair. Liturgy took place on the streets and not only in the churches. In describing the relation between religion and culture in late antique Byzantium, historian Peter Brown has put this same idea very well:

> Styles of liturgy and preaching show how easily the street flowed into the basilica; and the receding tide brought out much of the holy into the street.[10]

Our sources have shown that the city itself was employed as the scene for Christian worship. In one sense this liturgy of the streets was a means of

---

[8] Sozomen, *Ecclesiastical History* VIII:8. A readily available English translation of Sozomen by Chester D. Hartraupt is available in *A Select Library of Nicene and Post-Nicene Fathers of the Christian Church*, second series, eds. Philip Schaff and Henry Wace (New York: Christian Literature Company, 1890).

[9] Juan Mateos, *La célébration de la parole dans la liturgie byzantine*, Orientalia Christiana Analecta 191 (Rome: Pont. Institutum Orientalium Studiorum, 1971), pp. 34–38; R. Taft, "How Liturgies Grow: the Evolution of the Byzantine 'Divine Liturgy,'" *Orientalia Christiana Periodica* 43 (1977): 364–65.

[10] Peter Brown, "Eastern and Western Christianity in Late Antiquity: A Parting of the Ways," ed. Derek Baker, *Studies in Church History* 12 (1976): 20–21.

religious propaganda, advocating the superiority of one or another ecclesiastical party. But eventually this type of public worship also showed that
urban society and the religious faith that was its underpinning were inextricably intertwined. For the medieval Byzantine, worship was not a matter
of personal idiosyncrasy or private taste, confined to the walls of a building; it
was a manifestation of the culture itself.

In this same vein one must note the importance of public plazas for
liturgical celebrations. In forty-six of the sixty-eight liturgical processions
that we have identified in the *Typikon* of the Great Church, there was a
special service in the city's main plaza, the Forum of Constantine. In terms of
urban religious life, then, this Forum was nearly as important as the Great
Church itself.

III. A City Sanctified by Worship

Over the so-called Beautiful Doors of the southwest vestibule of Hagia
Sophia, an entrance regularly used by the emperor and his retinue, a tenth-
century mosaic shows the Mother of God seated on a throne with the child
Jesus on her lap. She is receiving two gifts. On her left stands the Emperor
Justinian holding his rebuilt Great Church. On the right stands the Emperor
Constantine with his gift to the Virgin, the city of Constantinople itself. Few
representations could so well manifest the idea of Constantinople. It was (at
least from the seventh century on) considered to be dedicated to Mary, the
Theotokos, the Mother of God. Moreover, it was dedicated entirely—not just
its shrines and churches, but the whole city.

In return, of course, the Mother of God was the major protector of the
city. Her most sacred relics (there were no bodily relics according to the
tradition that her body had been assumed into heaven at her death) were her
robe and her cincture. These Constantinople possessed and kept at the
shrines of Blachernae and Chalkoprateia respectively. Symbolically it was
she who assumed the posture of the city's main military defender, as the
following *troparion*, employed twice in the Lenten liturgy, shows:

> You have provided our city with an unvanquishable rampart, the Virgin
> who bore you, O Savior, through her save our souls, we pray you, from
> the dangers that assail us all about. (*Typikon* 2.52,58)

It was the Virgin who saved the city several times in the seventh century
and then again in the ninth century, as the Patriarch Photius made clear in
two of his homilies on the siege of the Rus in 860. In the first he excoriated
the populace for being lax in their attendance at liturgical services, except of
course when their lives were in danger. In the second homily he described
what happened when the Virgin's robe was taken out of its special chapel at
Blachernae to repulse the Russian invaders:

> When the whole city was carrying with me her raiment for the repulse
> of the besiegers and protection of the besieged we offered freely our
> prayers and performed the litany [i.e., in procession], thereupon with
> ineffable compassion she spoke out in motherly intercession. . . . Truly
> is the most holy garment the raiment of God's Mother. It embraced the
> walls, and the foes inexplicably showed their backs; the city put it
> around itself, and the camp of the enemy was broken up as at a signal;
> the city bedecked itself with it. . . .[11]

Not only did relics of the Mother of God act as special protection devices
for the city, but the very positioning of shrines dedicated to her manifest the
idea of the Virgin Mary as the city's protective patroness. Among the one
hundred-twenty-three shrines, churches, and monasteries that Raymond
Janin lists for Constantinople, several stand out as protective shrines.[12] Just
as the martyrial shrines of Peter, Paul, and Lawrence encircled Rome, so did
the shrines of the Mother of God at Blachernae, located at the very northern
tip of the city, at the Palaia Petra, just north of the Adrianople Gate, and the
Pege (the Virgin of the Miraculous Source), located to the northwest of the
Golden Gate. Each of these (and most often Blachernae) acted as a terminus
for liturgical processions (i.e., supplications for the city and its inhabitants)
during the course of the church year. In addition to the Mother of God,
Constantinople had two other protectors, John the Apostle and John the
Baptist, both of whom had shrines at the Hebdomon along the Via Egnatia to
Rome.

We should not underestimate the drawing power of these shrines. They
were not merely located in pleasant surroundings outside the city walls
(Constantinople always had plenty of open green space within the Theodosian Walls); they also symbolized divine protection for the city itself. As early
as the fourth century Jerome could say, "Movetur urbs sedibus suis," "the
city has changed its very location"[13]—so popular were the shrines of the saints
containing their powerful relics or attesting astounding miracles. It is only
with slight exaggeration that Peter Brown has recently written: "Late antique
Christianity, as it impinged on the outside world, *was* shrines and relics."[14]
This held true throughout the medieval period as well. Constantinople had a
"manifest destiny," because it was protected by supernatural defenders. The
urban liturgy repeatedly reminded the population of this fact.

Constantinople was the very heart of the Byzantine Empire. Even when

[11] Cyril Mango, trans. *The Homilies of Photius, Patriarch of Constantinople*, Dunbarton
Oaks Studies 9 (Washington, D.C.: Dunbarton Oaks Research Library and Collection,
1958), p. 102.

[12] Raymond Janin, *La géographie écclésiastique de l'empire byzantine*, 2d ed. (Paris:
Institut français d'etudes byzantines, 1969), 3 *(Les églises et les monastères)*: entry
"Theotokos."

[13] Jerome, *Epistle* 107.1.

[14] Peter Brown, *The Cult of the Saints: Its Rise and Function in Latin Christianity*
(Chicago: University of Chicago Press, 1981), p. 12.

there was precious little empire to be capital over, it was *the* city, and without it there could be nothing like an empire, as the emperors in exile found out in Nicaea and Trebizond after the Latin conquest of 1204. The city itself was the symbol of an eschatological vocation, for it had been entrusted with keeping the true faith alive until the end of time.[15] Of course, all cities in the ancient and medieval worlds were held together by some sort of ideology of the sacred. All of them, right from the very beginnings of history, centered their urban social life on the sacred.[16] In a particular way, however, the urban liturgy of Constantinople was intimately tied to the sacredness of the city and to the idea of divine protection. It was due to this close tie, as well as to the city's political centrality, that the liturgy of Constantinople was so influential on all the Greek churches and their descendants.

Through the liturgical use and the dynamic interplay of churches, streets, plazas, and extraurban spaces, the entire city became something like a church. By its very structure the liturgy of Constantinople identified the participants as inhabitants of a sacred city. Urban worship, therefore, was part of the seamless whole of life in medieval Constantinople. It was an indispensable factor for a society that considered itself special and sacred, protected by God and by the Mother of God. Not unlike modern urban dwellers, the people of Constantinople called their city "The City." And they called themselves *Romaioi,* the inheritors of the first Rome. For their predecessors, *civitas* meant not only walls, buildings, streets, and social relationships; it connoted civilization itself. For the medieval Byzantine, this *civitas* was inconceivable without worship at its most public.

---

[15] Cyril Mango, *Byzantium: The Empire of New Rome* (London: Weidenfeld and Nicolson, 1980), pp. 201–17; Robert Browning, *The Byzantine Empire* (New York: Scribner, 1980), p. 96; Peter Brown, *The Cult of the Saints,* pp. 92–93.

[16] Lewis Mumford, *The City in History* (New York: Harcourt, Brace & World, 1961), p. 68.

Part Two

6

Nightmare and Dream:
The Earthly City in Dante's *Commedia*

PETER S. HAWKINS
Yale Divinity School

In *Paradiso* 8 Dante and his guide Beatrice are suddenly translated into the celestial sphere of Venus, where one might well expect that heavenly conversation would turn itself to talk of love. Yet Dante's initial encounter with this particular company of heaven is concerned not with *eros* but with *civitas*, and in particular with the calamities that occur when those who have been blessed providentially with the ability to govern give up their leadership to others who have only the lust (but not the gift) for power. Dante speaks there with the soul of Charles Martel, whose family, the Angevins, he held responsible for much of the "mala segnoria," or bad rule, that kept Italy in a state of social and political nightmare. It is in the midst of their talk about the sad realities of sweet seed bearing bitter fruit, of things going from good to bad to worse, that Martel asks Dante a question so radical that it brings us to the heart of the poem's assumptions about the civic order. "Now say," he asks, "would it be worse for man on earth if he were not a citizen?" ("Or dì: sarebbe il peggio / per l'omo in terra, se non fosse cive?" 8.115–116).[1]

The question is direct, but not simple. To begin with, it is posed somewhat tortuously as a kind of double negative—would it be *worse* if man were *not*—as if to reflect in syntax the dark realities of life *in terra*. Then there is the word which Martel uses here for "citizen," not the customary Italian *cittadina*, but rather *cive*, a Latinism that evokes both the antique world of civic humanism, as well as Dante's own brand of neoclassicism: his dream of a world citizenry united under the universal *imperium* of a just monarch. It was this very dream that Dante accused Martel's family of systematically undermining through their opposition to Henry VII of Luxembourg, the man whom Dante hailed as the "one who is to come."[2]

---

[1] All citations of the *Commedia* are taken from *The Divine Comedy*, translated, with a commentary, by Charles S. Singleton, Bollingen Series 80 (Princeton: Princeton University Press, 1970–75).

[2] Dante's hopes for Henry VII, and the messianic rhetoric with which he heralded his

The question Martel poses, in other words, prepares us for a reply that will be as dense (and perhaps as fraught) as the question itself. Yet the reader's expectations of a witty or ironic rejoinder are utterly foiled, for what Dante offers his heavenly questioner is an unmitigated affirmation of our identity as political animals. Would it be worse for man on earth if he were not a citizen? "Yes," he answers, "and here I seek no proof." (" 'Sì,' rispuos' io; 'e qui ragion non cheggio,' " 8.117.) Whatever the actualities of civic life on earth, no matter how unrealized their potential or perverted their expression, it is still better to be a citizen, a member of a community, than not.

The terrible poignancy of this affirmation is that Dante wrote these lines (even as he wrote the whole of the *Commedia*) in exile. He was a man without a home, going from one Italian city-state to another, and looking back at Florence, the city that had unjustly banished him, with a mixture of wrath and of longing. He was, in other words, a man who knew firsthand just how much worse it is on earth *not* to be a citizen. In the opening treatise of the *Convivio*, written in the early years of his exile, we get perhaps our sharpest impression of what it meant for someone as rooted as Dante in the life of a particular community to become, for all intents and purposes, a displaced person: "Wandering as a stranger through almost every region to which our language reaches, I have gone about as a beggar, showing against my will the wound of fortune. . . . Verily I have been as a ship without sails and without rudder, driven to various harbours and shores by the dry wind which blows from pinching poverty."[3] When he later set the narrative action of his *Commedia* in spring of 1300, he placed his journey through the afterlife two years before this desperate wandering actually began. Nonetheless, it is present throughout the poem in prophecy, as Dante-pilgrim slowly learns what Dante-poet had already come to know, painfully, in his own flesh: the displeasures of always eating food that tastes a little "foreign"; the hardness of climbing up and down another person's stairs; the terrible loneliness of being a party by oneself, a constituency of one.[4]

---

coming to Italy, are seen in Epistolae 5–7, *Dantis Alagherii Epistolae*, ed. and trans. Paget Toynbee (Oxford: Clarendon Press, 1920). Compare the tone of these letters with the *Commedia's* last reference to "alto Arrigo" in *Par.* 30.133–38, quite obviously written after the death of Henry at Buonconvento in August of 1313.

[3] *Convivio* 1.3.5. "[Per] le parti quasi tutte a le quali questa lingua si stende, peregrino, quasi mendicando, sono andato, mostrando contra mia voglia la piaga de la Fortuna. . . . Veramente io sono stato legno sanza velo e sanza governo, portato a diversi porti e foci e liti dal vento secco che vapora la dolorosa povertade. . ." *Il Convivio*, ed. G. Busnelli and G. Vandelli, 2 vols. (Firenze: Felice Le Monnier, 1934). English translation by Dorothy Sayers, in *The Comedy of Dante Alighieri the Florentine, Hell* (Harmondsworth, Middlesex: Penguin Books, 1949; 1975), p. 39.

[4] I am alluding here to the prophecy of Dante's future put into the mouth of Cacciaguida in *Par.* 17.55–69. For a discussion of the significance of Dante's becoming a party of one ("Fatta parte per te stesso," 1.69), see Edward Peters, *"Pars, Parte:* Dante and an Urban Contribution to Political Thought" in *The Medieval City*, ed. Harry A. Miskimin, et. al., (New Haven: Yale University Press, 1977), pp. 113–40.

Given this displacement, it is all the more poignant that the great poem which emerges from this homeless "state" of alienation should be nothing less than an epic exploration of what Dante himself lacked when he wrote it: *civitas,* the reality of being a citizen in community. But like Milton in his blindness, presented by nature with a "universal blank" and yet conjuring through language a world of light, so too in his *Commedia* Dante by virtue of sheer verbal sway presides over an imperial realm of civic realities. It is between those realities that the pilgrim makes his typological journey from Egypt to Jerusalem (*Par.* 25.55–56), and among them that implicitly the reader is asked to choose. Thus, the absence of Dante's own city becomes the presence of the poem: a diverse commonwealth of social worlds encircled by its own hundred canto walls, a "word city"[5] built out of *terza rima,* from whose vantage the poet might both wage his war against the world and tender his peace.

Guiding the builder's hand in this massive work of civic reflection and construction is the magisterial influence of Augustine's *City of God.* This is not to deny Dante's vastly different estimate of Rome, Virgil, and the positive prospects of the political order; it is to say, rather, that Augustine offered him a profoundly psychological notion of *civitas* that seems not only to explain something of the world of the poem, but also to have generated some of its major images. Defining community as a shared object of love, Augustine's great paradigm is the *civitas Dei* in heaven, the city as it was first created and meant to be, wherein each creature, be it angel or human, finds in God the ultimate object of desire and therefore the common bond with everyone else. What he describes is a commonwealth "in which there is no love of a will that is personal or, so to speak, private, but a love that rejoices in a good that is at once shared by all and unchanging—a love that makes 'one heart' out of many, a love that is the wholehearted and harmonious obedience of mutual affection," (15.3).[6] Because this mutuality of self with self is grounded in an adoration of the city's divine ruler, Augustine can even go so far as to suggest that the blessed experience the beatific vision of God by seeing Him "face to face" in the faces of one another, "spiritually perceived by each one of us in each one of us, perceived in one another, perceived by each in himself" (22.29).[7]

The parody of this divine paradigm, which in fact offers a total inversion

---

[5] For the notion of a "word city" as opposed to a "real city" I am indebted to Burton Pike, *The Image of the City in Modern Literature* (Princeton: Princeton University Press, 1981). The distinction between the two is presented in the preface, pp. ix–xiv.

[6] "ubi sit non amor propriae ac privatae quodam modo voluntatis sed communi eodemque immutabili bono gaudes atque ex multis unum cor faciens, id est perfecte concors oboedientia caritatis." *The City of God Against the Pagans,* ed. and trans. Philip Levine (Cambridge: Harvard University Press, 1966). The English translation is by Henry Bettenson, in *Concerning the City of God Against the Pagans,* ed. David Knowles (Harmondsworth, Middlesex: Penguin Books, 1972).

[7] "Deus nobis erit notus atque conspicuus, ut videatur spiritu a singulis nobis in singulis nobis, videatur ab altero in altero, videatur in se ipso. . . ."

of it, is the *civitas diaboli*. First chartered in Satan's refusal to love God in order to love himself, this city of the devil is a contradiction in terms, a non-city. For just as evil is for Augustine the privation of good, so is the *civitas diaboli* the negation of *civitas*. This is because each citizen of its realm, having followed Satan in making the supreme act of self-choice, becomes in effect the ultimate object of his or her own love. The result of this auto-idolatry is that there can be no single God, no common bond or allegiance, no mutual affection, no corporate identity. The end of *amor sui* is total atomization, its politics an endless warfare of one would-be sovereign self against every other in a struggle for control and supremacy.

Although both the *civitas Dei* and the *civitas diaboli* are eternal kingdoms, Augustine is preoccupied with the contending roles they play in the history of the earthly city, that temporal, transitory battleground between heaven and hell—which is invariably presented by him as if hell, in fact, had the upper hand. Unlike Eusebius, there is no sense in Augustine that with the formal Christianization of the empire, heaven had begun its descent to earth. Rather, he treats the *civitas terrena* of this day not only as pagan, but as in direct continuity with that first human city founded by Cain, which (like Satan) gives itself to itself throughout the ages (15.7), aiming at the domination of others but finally overcome by its own lust for dominion. But if Augustine confuses the earthly city with the *civitas diaboli*, so that the two often seem to be synonymous with one another, he does not go so far as actually to identify them. This is partly because, even in their fallen condition, human communities (like human individuals) retain vestiges of the divine image. But more importantly, it is because the earthly city, if dominated by Satanic self-love, is also the place wherein the city of God is at work recruiting its citizens-elect, transforming the children of Cain into fellow travellers with Abel: men and women who pray for the peace of Babylon, but who live there only in body, being in heart and mind pilgrims en route to the heavenly Jerusalem. Therefore, while the eternal realms of heaven and hell are clear and distinct in their fundamental opposition, Augustine's picture of the earthly city (despite his rhetoric) must of necessity be a blur—a turbulence of forces sweeping through the confusion of history toward the sharp focus of eternity.[8]

This Augustinian schema of rival notions of *civitas* provided Dante with a groundplan for the *Commedia*, a set of civic and theological abstractions that he would bring vividly to life in his imagined survey of "the state of the soul after death." Beginning with the infernal parody, he leads us through a series of three concentric cityscapes, each funneling downward to the abyss of self-love as one by one we witness the undoing of all the ties that bind us together, until, at the center of hell and at the bottom of the universe, we see

---

[8] For a study of this "confusion" in Augustine's thought about the *civitas terrena*, see my "Polemical Counterpoint in *De Civitate Dei*," *Augustinian Studies* 6 (1975): 97–106.

the ruler of this "città dolente" engaged in an eternal act of cannibalism. He is the *libido dominandi* of this anticity, incarnate and in action. But it is not with him, or with what Dorothy Sayers has called the "miserific" vision, that we are meant to end.[9] Rather, the goal of the poem is to bring us to that positive reality of which all hell has been but the negative. It is in the final *cantica*, therefore, that we discover the paradigm that hell had so perversely parodied. Dante's city of God is a place of many revelations, and not the least among them has to do with the deepest reality of *civitas* itself. For it is in paradise that we come to see how the ideal of community expressed by Augustine—the unity in diversity, the one heart shared by different persons, the mutuality of affection—is nothing less than the divine life of the Trinity Himself, the three in one and one in three, who is imaged and echoed throughout the vast structure of the poem. *Paradiso* is the sounding of this mystery: the mystery that God is Himself a transcendent commonwealth of persons, a community of lovers, who calls the blessed to discover their own citizenship in Him.

Where Dante enriches the Augustinian model is in his exploration of how the civic parody may be converted into the paradigm; or, to use the anachronism of photography, how the negative image can be developed. For whereas Augustine was primarily concerned to contrast the city of darkness with the city of light, Dante is more openly interested in the process of enlightenment, of darkness turning into light. This is not to say that the *civitas diaboli* we find conjured up by *Inferno* is capable of any kind of transformation, for it is fixed forever in the prison of self-choice, frozen within the circuit of its own boundaries. But the antisocial realities which it statically, eternally represents can, when confronted in the fluid realm of history, be rejected. For those who make the disavowal before their death, there remains the working out of precisely that decision: the unlearning of one city's ways and the discovery of another's. It is this transformation that Dante gives us in the *Purgatorio:* his vision of how the children of Cain who reject their forefather's legacy come in the afterlife to complete their identification with Abel. Thus the mountain of Purgatory on which the penitents make their gradual ascent, while not itself a city, is a kind of naturalization center, a transitional place where one learns to become a citizen of heaven. It is there that the soul is cured of self-love and freed instead to discover the true end of its desire. Whereas hell funnels downward, Purgatory spirals up, bringing its immigrants to the point where they can assume their new citizenship. It brings them to a beginning, and yet in a strange way it is also a coming home. For once enabled to return to Eden at the summit of the mountain—to reenter the great nest from which all humankind was expel-

---

[9] The phrase is clearly meant to suggest the type-countertype relationship between the cities of hell and heaven, with each city centered in a self-revealing moment of vision, miserific or beatific. See Dorothy Sayer's essay, "The City of Dis," in *Introductory Papers on Dante* (New York: Harper and Brothers, 1954), pp. 127–50.

led—those who have completed their purgation are ready to enter into that mature partnership with God which Adam and Eve failed to grow into. It is a union that Dante portrays in *Paradiso* as the wedding of garden and city, as the end for which our earthly beginning was made.[10]

The reader's attention throughout this survey of a *civitas* lost, regained, and enjoyed is centered on the figure of Dante. He is the living man with whom we can identify even under the extraordinary circumstances of a journey beyond the grave, and in whose experience the poet hopes we too can participate—and not only for the pleasures of the text. This is to say that despite the otherworldly nature of the poem's itinerary, its strategy and concerns are profoundly oriented to this world. To begin with, the pilgrim is no allegorical Everyman, but rather someone radically connected to time and place, to a network of specific persons, political controversies and ephemera. (Such is the stuff of which footnotes are made!) Then there is the trajectory of the poem itself, its designs on the consciousness of the reader who lives (and reads) with the possibility of choice and, therefore, with the opportunity to take a spiritual pilgrimage of his or her own—a pilgrimage to be carried out within this world.[11]

Perhaps most of all, however, the poem convinces us of its solid grounding in our experience because it has as its central frame of reference the city of earth in its successive historical manifestations and in all its symbolic ambivalence, mythic resonance, and local color. For it is through Thebes and Troy and Rome, through the urban landscape of Trecento Italy, and through Florence above all that we are enabled to conceive the worlds of the poem. This is partly a matter of sheer metaphoric necessity, for how else could Dante envision the civic realities that no one has ever seen except through the lens of the cities we know, either firsthand or through literary tradition? The effect of this complexity of simile and cross-reference (which is especially intense in the *Inferno*) is to do more than provide metaphoric access to an imagined cosmography of the beyond. It suggests that in addition to depicting "the state of the soul after death," the poem is exploring the earthly city itself as a place of damnation, transformation and beatitude. This is not to say that Dante viewed the *civitas terrena* as any more permanent than did Augustine; together with history, it will be rolled up like a scroll.[12] But if not permanent, it is nonetheless polyvalent: not simply a place where one chooses one's eternal citizenship, but a place to experience proleptically the civic orders of the life to come—for better or for worse.

---

[10] For Dante's final conflation of garden and city in *Paradiso*, see A. Bartlett Giamatti, *The Earthly Paradise and the Renaissance Epic* (Princeton: Princeton University Press, 1966), pp. 94–119, esp. pp. 116–19.

[11] For the reading of the *Commedia* as an *itinerarium mentis* in our world, see Charles Singleton, *Journey to Beatrice* (Baltimore: The John Hopkins University, 1977), pp. 4–14.

[12] Augustine's image of the temporal order as a scroll to be rolled up is found in *Confessions* 13.15.

Dante's experience of the worst shows itself with a vengeance in the pages of *Inferno,* where the hell-on-earth that he found among the warring city-states of Italy became his model for the *civitas diaboli.* It is a model which, furthermore, throws back its relentless judgment on the Italian "original" from which it is taken. For what do we see when we pass through the gates of Dis but the grotesque portrait of a medieval city, a hill town sucked in upon itself into a kind of massive sinkhole, so that its dark, narrow passageways wind down instead of leading up, finally bringing the traveller to Satan's travesty of a throneroom, a parody of Duomo and Signoria alike? In reading this first *cantica* we are continually asked to visualize its scene in terms of well-known Tuscan monuments or cityscapes; to meet former citizens of Pistoia, Pisa, and Lucca, as well as an innumerable host of Florentines; to find them still caught in the hatreds of faction and family and civic self-interest; to calculate the sheer havoc wrought on earth by the very same pride, envy, and avarice that make hell a place of horror and loathing.

As we descend closer to the bottom of this reality, it is the ancient city of Thebes that becomes the coordinating image of both the earthly and infernal, the exemplar of community possessed by the devil, whether it be aboveground or below.[13] Let me remind you briefly of its stories. Cadmus sows the dragon's teeth from which spring full grown men who no sooner gain consciousness than they begin to fight and kill one another. Five of the warriors survive, and from them descends a citizenry whose arrogance is based on their claim to have escaped the common origin of humankind. As the subsequent history of Thebes shows, however, the sowing of the dragon's teeth goes on to reap a civic whirlwind: the denial of human generation spawns a generational conflict that violates every limit of experience. Oedipus kills his father and has children with his mother; his sons then kill one another in a struggle to gain rulership. From their deadly fraternal conflict rise the Seven against Thebes whose sons, in turn, avenge the deaths of their fathers by destroying the city. Pentheus is torn limb from limb by his frenzied mother; Tydeus gnaws the head of his enemy Menalippus—and from the bloody accumulation of these horrors one can understand how Thebes served Dante as a mythic screen against which to project his own nightmare vision: a human city godless, arrogant, and self-destructive enough to be hell.

This essay is not the occasion to show how the poet makes use of this material over the long course of *Inferno.* For our purposes it will be enough to look at the culmination of these Theban references in cantos 32 and 33, where Ugolino tells the story of how he and his sons were nailed inside a tower dungeon by the Pisan Archbishop Ruggieri, until one by one the children dropped from hunger, and their father, driven mad by starvation,

---

[13] Dante's primary Theban sources were Statius' *Thebaid* and Ovid's *Metamorphoses,* Book 3. For his valorization of the city, see Giuseppi Mazzotta, *Dante, Poet of the Desert* (Princeton: Princeton University Press, 1979), pp. 98–99.

fell upon their corpses "when fasting did more than grief had done." Midway in this narration Ugolino asks what one could possibly weep over if not over this tale; there is, in fact, nothing in the entire poem to match it. And yet Dante shows the storyteller to be no innocent, but rather a traitor among traitors, punished for his own sins against the human community. Although allowed by the grim justice of hell to gnaw forever upon the skull of Archbishop Ruggieri, like Tydaeus upon the head of Menalippus, he is in fact hardly less depraved than the cleric who destroyed him. Therefore if Ugolino's story is full of pathos, it is not for him that we weep, but for the victims of a civic order that devours its own children, its enemies, and in the end itself. What the poet gives us in this glimpse of Pisa as "novella Tebe" is a dreadful fantasy of the *civitas terrena* actually becoming the *civitas diaboli*. It is as if the membrane of grace that mercifully divides the two realms might actually dissolve under the corrosive impact of earthly depravity. When we move from the Ugolino episode to our vision of Satan's cannibalism in the final canto of *Inferno*, it is with an enormous sense of anticlimax—as if in portraying the depths to which the earthly city can descend Dante had exhausted his resources for the depiction of evil.

If Pisa and her sister communes offer Dante his metaphor for hell—if they provide him with a model of anti-*civitas* overwhelmed by its own lust for domination—we neither leave their reality nor the poet's denunciation of it when we move on to purgatory and paradise. On the contrary, throughout the poem we are reminded that as it is in hell, so it is *in terra*. Thus, for instance, in the great prophetic lament of *Purgatorio* 6—"Ahi serva Italia"— Dante presents us once again with a brutal picture of the contemporary body politic at war with its own members:

> e ora in te non stanno sanza guerra
> li vivi tuoi, e l'un l'altro si rode
> di quei ch' un muro e una fossa serra. (6.82–84)

> and now in you your living abide
> not without war, and of those whom
> one wall and one moat shut in,
> one gnaws at the other!

Here we get another picture of Ugolino, in Pisa and in hell. Even as far along in the poem as *Paradiso* 30, when Beatrice shows Dante the assembled host of heaven with all the joy of one who is bringing someone home for the first time—"Vedi nostra città quant' ella gira" (30.130)—she turns suddenly from the radiant fellowship before her to describe the world which Dante has come from and to which he must return:

> La cieca cupidigia che v'ammalia
> simili fatti v'ha al fantolino
> che muor per fame e caccia via la balia. (30.139–141)

> The blind cupidity which bewitches you has

made you like the little child who dies
of hunger and drives away his nurse.

In both these images at once corporeal and alimentary—whether it be the evocation of gnawed flesh in *Purgatorio* 6 or the turned-from breast in *Paradiso* 30—the poet is suggesting the way in which the earthly city has rejected the transcendent notion of *civitas* presented in the Eucharist. Instead of "Take, eat, this is my body given for you," with its implications of a corporate identity for those who share in that meal together, we have, rather, an "eat or be eaten" world blindly devouring what will only destroy it, while at the same time repelling the nourishment that can save.[14]

But if this negative and essentially Augustinian assessment of the *civitas terrena* remains a constant shadow within the poem, casting its darkness even upon the effulgence of heaven, it is by no means the only evaluation Dante offers. Yet in order to find the positive image of earthly *civitas*, and with it the earthly hope, one must by and large turn away from the model of the city-state to that of the empire; turn, that is, from the demonic *urbs* to the *imperium* that embraces both city and world in peace. This movement matches the actual course of the pilgrim's journey as he leaves the claustrophobically walled-in city of *Inferno* for that heavenly empire of *Paradiso* which has only love and light for boundaries (28.54). It is the empire which Beatrice describes in the Garden of Eden as "quella Roma onde Cristo è romano" (*Purg.* 32.102), that Rome where Christ is a Roman, which Dante enters like a country bumpkin coming into the "eternal city" for the very first time:

> Se i barbari, venendo da tal plaga
> che ciascun giorno d'Elice si cuopra,
> rotante col suo figlio ond' ella e vaga,
>
> veggendo Roma e l'ardüa sua opra,
> stupefaciensi, quando Laterano
> a le cose mortali andò di sopra;
>
> io, che al divino da l'umano,
> a l'etterno dal tempo era venuto,
> e di Fiorenza in popol giusto e sano,
>
> di che stupor dovea esser compiuto! (31.31–40)

If the Barbarians, coming from such region as is covered every day by Helice, wheeling with her son whom she delights in, when they beheld Rome and her mighty work, when Lateran rose above all mortal things, were wonder-struck, I, who to the divine from the human, to the eternal from time had come, and from Florence to a people just and sane, with what amazement must I have been full!

[14] A brilliant reading of the Ugolino episode as a travesty of the eucharistic offering is given by John Freccero, "Bestial Sign and Bread of Angels (*Inferno* 32–33)," *Yale Italian Studies* 1 (1977): 53–66.

In choosing throughout *Paradiso* to represent the celestial realm in Roman metaphor rather than through the more traditional association with Jerusalem, Dante is, of course, reflecting the bias of his own political vision. He reveals his longing for the restoration of a supreme authority able first to control and then to unite the warring city-states of his day; a world government ordained by God to realize the potential for human happiness here on earth, in tandem with (but quite separate from) the church. This is what Rome meant for him, both as it existed under Augustus and as it might still more wondrously exist in the Christian era. The great irony here is that Augustine's Roman nightmare is Dante's Roman dream, for in the *Commedia* imperial *civitas* becomes nothing less than the civic metaphor for heaven and the redemptive option for earth. Through it Dante charts the rediscovery of unity in diversity, of one heart grown strong out of many, of citizens who mean "we" and "ours" when they say "I" and "mine" (to recall the imperial speech of the eagle of justice in *Paradiso* 19.11–12).

Dante's dream, of course, did not come true, and with the pathetic failure and death of Henry of Luxembourg in 1313 it must have seemed more and more to him (as it no doubt does to us) that the idea of empire which he longed for could only exist in the pages of *De Monarchia* or in that heavenly Rome, which is above and free, celebrated in the third *cantica* of the poem. What remained with him, writing the *Paradiso* in Ravenna right up until his death in 1321, was the fact of his exile and the continual discovery of his spiritual pilgrimage. To say this, however, should not be to confuse Dante's particular status as a resident alien with the spiritual rejection of the *civitas terrena* which we find exemplified in Augustine. For although he was a stranger and pilgrim in the world to a degree unknown to the very residential Bishop of Hippo; though he recognized that the civic order had become a dark wood in which to lose one's way (and possibly one's soul); though by his own poetic journey he turns our attention from human to divine, from time to eternity, from Florence to a people just and sane—despite all this, he remained convinced that *civitas* and *humanitas* are one, as much in this life as in the life to come.[15]

It would, in fact, be worse for a man on earth if he were not a citizen; indeed, he might cease to be human altogether. Therefore, it is in the context of an essential affirmation of the earthly city that we must consider Dante's bitter denunciations of it, even as he consigns its policies to hell and lambastes it up and down the afterlife. For rather than turning away in disgust after visiting a plague upon every house, he is instead like some Hebrew prophet shouting outside the gates of a Jerusalem that does not want to listen. He is like Hosea haranguing his whore of a wife and renaming their

---

[15] See Ernst Kantorowicz's discussion of Dante's notion of *humana civilitas*, with its promise of earthly as well as heavenly fulfillment, in *The King's Two Bodies, a Study in Medieval Political Theology* (Princeton: Princeton University Press, 1957), pp. 451–95.

children—anything to bring her back from the living death she has chosen, anything to recall her to her true self.

When Dante suggests what this identity may be, when he gives us a picture of that true self which the *civitas terrena* has abandoned, it is not only of Rome and empire that he speaks, but also of Florence, the earthly city that even the damned denounce—the city which one critic of the poem proposes as the civic model for hell.[16] To be sure, in order to show the parody become a paradigm, to see the hideous witch suddenly as a beautiful maiden, Dante must radically alter our perspective on Florence from the one which he has consistently led us to take. This is most notably done in *Paradiso* 15, where Cacciaguida, Dante's great-great-grandfather, takes us back in time to the Florence of the good old days of the early twelfth-century: a city living peacefully within its ancient walls, sober and chaste, offering "a citizen's life so peaceful and so fair, a community so loyal, a dwelling place so sweet" (15.130–32).[17] The contrast between then and now is, of course, part of Dante's point, for this hymn to the *civitas terrena* is also a lament for a paradise lost. From Cacciaguida he will learn in no uncertain terms of his future expulsion from Florence and the terrible honor it will bestow in forcing him to become a party by himself (17.69), a man without a city. The irony of the whole extended episode, moreover, is that Dante acquires in vivid detail a glorious heritage which he will shortly be unable to own. He learns more fully where he comes from only on the brink of losing that home.

Nonetheless, the idealized portrait of Florence which he gives us through Cacciaguida's memory is an idealization of *civitas* on earth. It is a godly city to be sure, but one which is, for all the nostalgia of the account, indisputably terrestrial and human. And it is to this human possibility that the poet turns our attention at the opening of *Paradiso* 25, where, after the pilgrim has successfully passed his examination in faith administered by none other than Saint Peter himself, the poet speaks to the reader directly, in his own exilic voice, about his own native city:

> Se mai continga che 'l poema sacro
> al quale ha posto mano e cielo e terra,

---

[16] Joan M. Ferrante, "Florence and Rome, The Two Cities of Man in *The Divine Comedy*" in *The Early Renaissance*, ed. Aldo S. Bernardo, *Acta* 5, Center for Medieval and Early Renaissance Studies (Binghampton: State University of New York, 1978), pp. 1–19. Ferrante expands upon this excellent paper in her recent book, *The Political Vision of the 'Divine Comedy'* (Princeton: Princeton University Press, 1984).

[17] Among the many fine discussions of the Cacciaguida episode are those offered by Fiorenzo Forti in *Enciclopedia Dantesca* (Roma: Istituto della Enciclopedia Dantesca, 1970), 1: 733–39, followed by a helpful bibliography; Giuseppi Mazzotta, *Dante, Poet of the Desert*, pp. 124–30; Raffaello Morghen, "Dante and the Florence of the Good Old Days" in *From Time to Eternity*, ed. Thomas G. Bergin (New Haven: Yale University Press, 1967), pp. 19–37; and Charles T. Davis, *Dante's Italy* (Philadelphia: University of Pennsylvania Press, 1984), pp. 71–93.

sì che m'ha fatto per molti anni macro,
vinca la crudeltà che fuor mi serra
del bello ovile ov'io dormi' agnello,
nimico ai lupi che li danno guerra;
con altra voce omai, con altro vello
ritornerò poeta, e in sul fonte
del mio battesmo prenderò 'l cappello;
però che ne la fede, che fa conte
l'anime a Dio, quivi intra' io. . . . (25.1–11)

If ever it come to pass that the sacred poem to which heaven and earth
have so set hand that it has made me lean for many years should
overcome the cruelty which bars me from the fair sheepfold where I
slept as a lamb, an enemy to the wolves which war on it, with changed
voice now and with changed fleece a poet I will return, and at the font of
my baptism will I take the crown; because there I entered into the Faith
that makes souls known to God. . . .

Although in this extraordinarily personal address to the reader Dante
looks backward, it is not over the course of four generations to the twelfth-
century fantasy described by Cacciaguida; it is, rather, to the Florence of his
own beginnings, the Florence to which he longs even now to return, however changed by age and suffering. In its succession of tenses the passage
joins memory and hope, past and future, to the poet's present act of writing.
In this way we see the extent to which Dante's personal history is defined in
terms of the city's continuity. As it was in the beginning, so, please God, may
it also be in the end: the city as the place in which to tell one's time. This
profound sense of temporal involvement between individual and community
is reinforced by the images of *civitas* he chooses here. For what he gives us
are circles of enclosure and incorporation, where sheepfold and font, urban
mass and pastoral flock, earthly citizenship and baptismal initiation are all
knit together into a dense notion of identity. This is the place where he
entered both life and faith: an earthly city that makes souls known to God. It
is Dante's civic version of Shakespheare's "other Eden, demi-paradise."

And yet as these same lines make clear, this city-as-Arcadia is perceived
within a fallen world, beset by the same wolves we have known since the first
canto of *Inferno* and governed by a cruelty so mad that it bars its gates to a
would-be shepherd willing to lay down his life for the sheep. It is as if there
were actually two cities superimposed, the one upon the other, and occupying the same physical *urbs:* a sheepfold of God's own lambs and a pen of
voracious predators. It is to the latter reality that this enemy of wolves
tirelessly draws our attention throughout the length of the *Commedia,* and
yet it is because of the former that he continues to make his suit, canto after
canto, even as he grows old and thin in the process. Therefore, while the
"sacred poem" seems most often to be a prolonged war against Florence, it is
on a deeper level a fight on behalf of the earthly city, an attempt to free it
from the wolves within.

Florence, of course, was not interested in Dante's peculiar forms of liberation. The poem proved to be no passport home, nor did the font of the poet's baptism turn out to be the scene of his coronation. But if Dante died in exile, as a party of one, the comedy he constructed out of personal tragedy provided him with a genuine way to be a citizen. It gave him the means to exercise what he understood to be the vocation of citizenship. Through the forum of his *Commedia* he could address the sheepfold which cruelty had barred against him, recalling the earthly city to that divine *civitas* which is its birthright and which it might still come to reveal.

7

"Fourteenth-Century Siena: The Iconography of a Medieval Commune"

DUNCAN ROBINSON
Yale University

In 1260, Sienese troops secured an unexpected advantage over the much larger army fielded by their enemies, the Florentines. The battle of Montaperti was a short-lived victory, an isolated incident in the long and ultimately unsuccessful campaign to establish imperial power among the fragmented local governments of the Italian peninsula. Inevitably, in the shifting sands of medieval politics, the conflict was exploited by individual city-states such as Florence and Siena to vent traditional and often intensely local rivalries. Florentine dignity was restored six years later. At Beneventum their troops not only crushed the transalpine ambitions of the imperial claimant Manfred; they also asserted the supremacy of Florence over her neighboring Tuscan rivals.

On the eve of the battle of Montaperti, the apprehensive Sienese gathered to perform one of those spontaneous acts of corporate worship for which the chroniclers of the Middle Ages have made the period famous. The account is that of Niccolò di Giovanni di Francesco Ventura.

> And whilst my Lord the Bishop with all the religious and clergy were thus going in procession, singing their litanies and prayers, God did put it into the mind of the syndic, that is to say of Buonaguida Lucari, to rise, and say in a voice so loud that he was heard by citizens who were outside the church in the piazza of S. Cristofano, "My lords of Siena, and my fellow citizens, we have already commended ourselves to King Manfred, now it appears to me that we ought in all sincerity to give ourselves, our goods and our persons, the city and the *contado*, to the Queen of Life Eternal, that is to say to our Lady Mother, the Virgin Mary. To make this offering let it be your pleasure to bear me company."
>
> And no sooner had he said these words than this Buonaguida stripped himself to his shirt. And, being barefooted and bareheaded, he

took his leathern girdle and fastened it around his neck with a slip-knot.
And in this guise, at the head of a procession of citizens, he set out
towards the Duomo. And behind him went all the people; and whom-
soever met them by the way went with them, each man being shoeless
and without cloak or hat . . . And as they went they ceased not to
cry,"Mary Virgin, succour us in our great need, and deliver us out of the
claws of these lions . . ."[1]

Needless to say, when victory in the field fell on the following day to the
outnumbered Sienese, a large measure of the credit was given to the divine
protectress of the city. Thereafter Siena defended with pride that special
relationship which gave to its insignia the initials C. S. C. V.: *Comune
Senarum Civitas Virginis*.

The incident is interesting in a number of ways. It illustrates the
interrelationship of church and state which typifies the medieval commune,
an interrelationship spelled out further in the civic statues of 1262.[2] In one
way these represented a formalization of secular authority, but in many of
their provisions, such as the statutes which defined the responsibilities of the
state toward the upkeep of the church and its religious orders, they demonstrate the interdependence of religious and secular authority. The civic
treasury was located in the sacristy of the church of San Cristofano—the
church before which Lucari rallied the citizenry in 1260—and the accounts
of the city were audited by trusted monks from the nearby convent of San
Galgano. Finally, the keys of the city were kept, for reasons of security, in the
cathedral dedicated to the Virgin; this was both a practical move and a
symbolic one which involved the divine protectress of Siena directly in the
safety of the city. The cathedral, then, was much more than the principal
ecclesiastical building; it was where the *Comune Senarum* became, by
corporate dedication and sustained devotion, the *Civitas Virginis*. As a focal
point for civic pride there was to be apparently no limit. In 1315, extensions
to the existing building were mooted to provide a new baptistry and choir;
these were superceded in 1329 by a far more ambitious scheme for a new
nave. Its gigantic columns, abandoned and built into later structures, stand
today as evidence of Sienese ambitions for their shrine of the Virgin.

It is against this background that a number of important commissions
need to be set. From 1284 until 1298 the famous sculptor Giovanni Pisano
served as *operaio*. To these years belong, presumably, his designs for the
cathedral's pulpit, in addition to its facade. Shortly afterwards, in 1308, the
painter Duccio di Buoninsegna was commissioned to execute an altarpiece
for the high altar (Figure A). There could have been no question about the

---

[1] Fifteenth-century mss., translated and quoted at length by Robert Langton Douglas,
History of Siena (London: J. Murray, 1902), p. 84f. For other references to the social and
political history of Siena, see Ferdinand Schevill, *Siena, The History of a Medieval
Commune* (New York: C. Scribner's Sons, 1909).

[2] E. Armstrong, "The Sienese Statutes of 1262," *English History Review* 15 (1900): 1–19.

subject matter of the principal panel. Traditional iconography had already established in Tuscan painting the convention of the Virgin and Child, usually enthroned, flanked by saints appropriate to the particular church and its state. Given the dual role of the Virgin in Siena, queen both of heaven and of the city, any deviation from this convention was unthinkable. Moreover, the Sienese Duccio had already distinguished himself in competition not only with local artists, but with the leading painters of central Italy. In the church of Santa Maria Novella in Florence, his Rucellai Madonna of 1285 consciously rivalled Cimabue's slightly earlier Santa Trinità Madonna. Together, they constituted the challenge to which Giotto was to rise, with his Ognissanti Madonna of c. 1300, but by comparison with which neither of the earlier panels is diminished.

The commission for the *Maestà* is one of the most specific documents of its kind to survive. It was drawn up by the Capomaestro of the cathedral, who was careful to detail the artist to use only the finest materials, to refuse other commissions until it was completed, and to devote to it the best of his skill.[3] This was not idle rhetoric. The workshop system of production allowed for considerable assistance besides outright subcontracting of work; the cathedral authorities were acting wisely when they attempted to establish both cost and quality control. Two years later, further instructions were issued in an attempt to speed up the work. The commissioners may have felt that the painter was relying a little too heavily on the piecework rates they had negotiated to provide a steady income. But in any event, by 1311 the painting was ready for delivery. "Painting" is, perhaps, misleading as a description of the vast complex of panels which constituted the altarpiece. Painted on both sides, with pinnacles and predella in addition to the main field, and a succession of small scenes illustrating the Gospel narrative on the reverse, the Sienese *Maestà* has been compared with some justice to the sculptural program of an entire cathedral facade.[4] For Duccio, it was an undisputed triumph in which he demonstrated that the art of panel painting was in no way inferior to that of fresco when it came to the narrative cycles. There is evidence to suggest that Duccio's success continued to redound to the credit of Sienese artists for several decades to follow. Some fifteen years later the Franciscans of Florence turned to a younger Sienese painter, Ugolino di Neri, for the high altarpiece of the church of Santa Croce—a church otherwise distinguished by the fresco decorations of Giotto and his immediate followers.

For the city of Siena, the completion of Duccio's *opera maravigliosa* gave opportunity for celebration, as well as for renewed devotion to the

---

[3] The Sienese state archive which gives the commission for the *Maestà*, Parchment 603 (9 October 1308), is quoted by John White, *Duccio, Tuscan Art and the Medieval Workshop* (London: Thames and Hudson, 1979), p. 192.

[4] *Ibid*, p. 102.

Virgin. The account of the procession with which the *Maestà* was carried
from Duccio's studio near the Porta Stalloreggia to the cathedral recalls the
more somber occasion of fifty years earlier:

> the shops were all closed, and bishop ordered a great and devout
> company of priests and friars to attend in procession the Signori Nove,
> and all the officials of the city and all the people; and all the greatest
> citizens in order of rank, with lighted candles in their hands, escorted
> the picture up to the cathedral, after proceeding around the Campo,
> according to custom, and all the bells rang loudly in honor of such a
> great and noble painting.[5]

Once again, a corporate act of worship combined civic pride with religious
fervor, while the inscription painted around the base of the Virgin's throne
took the form of a plea entered by the citizenry before their ultimate ruler:
"Mater Sancta Dei sis causa Senis requiei."

Pride in the embellishment of the cathedral was to continue for centuries. To the fifteenth century belong the elaborately inlaid pavements, the
frescoes of Pinturicchio in the Libreria Piccolomini, and the contributions of
Ghiberti, Donatello and Jacopo della Quercia to the decoration of the font in
the new baptistry. By 1311, however, construction of a new (and specifically
civic) building was under way. In common with other central Italian city-
states, and as a direct reflection of the growing complexity of local government, the Sienese embarked upon the erection of the Palazzo Pubblico, or
city hall. In 1310 the left wing of the new administration block was completed sufficiently for the elected rulers of the city to install their audience
chamber, chapel and offices. The bell tower which completes the profile of
the palace was begun in 1325, and capped after a design provided by the
painter, Lippo Memmi, in 1344. Meanwhile, during roughly the same
thirty-year period, the interior walls offered to local artists an opportunity for
fresco decoration unparalleled in even the largest of the city's churches and
monastic foundations.

The first commission for the new public building went to Lippo
Memmi's brother-in-law, Simone Martini. A younger artist than Duccio, and
almost certainly trained in his workshop, Simone was the choice of the city's
rulers when they set about the decoration of the council chamber. In his
fresco of 1315 he represented the Virgin as queen, together with her heavenly courtiers (Figure B). Artistically, the design provides a highly intelligent
and respectful development from the continuous ground evident in the main
panel of Duccio's *Maestà*. In his frescoed version of the same subject,
Simone exploited to the full the opportunity presented by the end wall of the
audience chamber. By means of the painted canopy overhead, he succeeded
in creating the illusion of distance beyond the surface of the wall. Sur-

---

[5] Anonymous Sienese chronicler of the mid-fourteenth century, published by Lodovico
Antonio Muratori, *Rerum italicarum scriptores*, 15, part 6 (Bologna: N. Zanichelli, 1931–
39), p. 90.

rounded and defined by pictorial space, the court of heaven is given the kind of physical presence which points forward to the trompe l'oeil effects exploited by Renaissance painters.

Didactically, the painting provides a dramatic embodiment of the dual role of the Virgin. From her eternal throne, she reigns not only over her divine subjects, but also over her terrestrial ones. Her court is represented in the council chamber as an upper house, beneath which the lawmakers of the *civitas Senarum* operate *sub species Virginis*. Through the inscription at her feet, she is made to speak of matters particular to her terrestrial subjects:

> Those angelic flowers, the rose and the lily with which the fields of heaven are strewn, are not more delightful to me than righteous counsel: But I see some who, for selfish ends, despise me and deceive my land, and are most praised when they speak worst. Woe unto him whom this speech condemns.[6]

Given the success of Simone's initial undertaking, it is not surprising that the Sienese government returned some years later to the same artist with a further, civic commission. Around 1327, the authorities decided to commemorate within the Palazzo Pubblico the achievements of Guidoriccio da Fogliano, a soldier of fortune who had served his commune against two of its rebellious dependencies (Figure C). The hill towns of Montemassi and Sassoforte are clearly recognizable in the background of the fresco that Simone produced. It is dominated, however, by the almost life-sized equestrian figure of the local hero, depicted in profile. The subject matter of this painted monument marks a radical departure from medieval conventions. Hitherto, as we have seen, the Sienese expressed civic ideals by means of religious iconography; their celebration of a living person has to be seen both politically and artistically as a challenging innovation. It is characteristic of Simone's artistic resourcefulness that, to answer the problem of representation which this commission posed, he looked backwards, beyond the confines of Christian iconography, to the classical tradition of imperial portraiture. The statue of Marcus Aurelius which stands now where Michelangelo sited it in the sixteenth century, in the Campidoglio in Rome, was during Simone's lifetime a few hundred yards away in the Forum. It had survived the iconoclasm of early Christian eras through mistaken identity:

---

[6] The Italian text of the inscription is as follows:

> L'angelichi fiorecti, rose e gigli
> onde s'adorna lo celeste prato
> non mi dilettan più che i buon consigli
> ma talor veggio che per proprio stato
> disprezza me a la mia tera inganna,
> e quando parla peggio è più lodato
> guardi ciascun cui questo dir condanna.

The English translation given in text is my own.

instead of the pagan emperor it actually represents, it was revered as an equestrian statue of the first Christian emperor, Constantine. For the fourteenth-century painter in search of new pictorial forms, it offered the perfect model, with its unmistakable references to military prowess and secular authority. The lead of Simone was to be followed in the next century by a number of Italian artists in conscious feats of classical revivalism: Donatello's statue of the Gattamelata at Padua, Uccello's painted tomb of Sir John Hawkwood in Florence and Castagno's rival monument to Niccolò da Tolentino. Once again, Simone emerges as an innovator worthy of the artistic challenges which Siena's civic commissions presented.

A very few years after the completion of the Guidoriccio fresco, the Sienese government began to contemplate a further cycle of frescoes with an overtly civic theme. Ambrogio Lorenzetti painted the frescoes of Good and Bad Government in the Sala dei Nove between 1337 and 1339. The commission to the painter, together with subsequent payments, is fully documented in the city's records.[7] There is no mention, on the other hand, of the source of the program or of the authorship of the lengthy verse inscriptions which may have helped the painter plan the decorations, even as they serve to interpret them for the spectator. The frescoes occupy three sides of a rectangular hall. On the central short wall facing the windows, an allegory of Good Government is represented (Figure D); the long wall to its right is devoted to two large, illustrative scenes of Good Government in the city and Good Government in the countryside. The opposing long wall to the left of the allegory of Good Government is divided between an allegory of Bad Government (Figure E) and, to its left, a vivid pictorial description of its effects upon town and country alike.

In his search for appropriate pictorial symbols, Ambrogio Lorenzetti was aided by the well-established medieval tradition of representations of vices and virtues. These often appeared as subsidiary figures in the great sculptural programs which adorned the facades of romanesque and gothic churches. There they were featured in the lower registers, as minor characters in the great spiritual histories of the Christian faith. Giotto incorporated such figures in his fresco cycle in the Arena Chapel in Padua, painted just after the turn of the fourteenth century and demonstrably known to Ambrogio Lorenzetti. In Giotto's allegory, the Vices and Virtues face one another across the private chapel built by Enrico Scrovegni, which he built in part to atone for his father's highly profitable sin of usury. They are painted in grisaille, itself a reminiscence of the carved reliefs from which the figures derive, seven on each side of the chapel, beneath the scenes of the lives of the Virgin and Child which constitute the main subject of the frescoes. Respectful of conventional iconography and appropriate to the theme of atonement, the

[7] Gaetano Milanesi, *Documenti dell' Arte Senese* (Siena: O. Porrti, 1854), 1: 195–96.

Last Judgment occupies the entire west wall, with Scrovegni himself depicted prominently as the donor whose gift ensures a smooth passage to heaven. The presence of the Vices and Virtues helps to underline the importance of Scrovegni's own pilgrimage toward salvation, a pilgrimage which is grounded in the varied reality of human experience. Significantly, Giotto's Vices and Virtues are not dominated, as one might expect, by the three "theological" virtues, Faith, Hope, and Charity. Instead, the central figures on each side of the chapel are Injustice and Justice respectively. This emphasis upon a distinctly social morality is borne out by the details. Injustice is depicted as a seated ruler, the fabric of society represented by the crumbling crenellated ruins that surround him, while at his feet a scene of armed robbery serves to demonstrate the state of anarchy over which he presides. It is as if the painter had set out to illustrate the words of St. Augustine in *City of God* 4.4, "If justice be removed, what are kingdoms but great bands of thieves?"

By contrast, Justice is a seated female figure, with more than a passing resemblance to Giotto's own Ognissanti Madonna. In her hands she holds the scales of justice, in which small angelic figures of reward and punishment balance each other on either side. At her feet, in opposition to the misrule of Injustice, the harmony of her influence is expressed by means of three carefully posed figures, frozen in the poses of a formal dance. The importance of Giotto's representation of Justice was not lost on Ambrogio Lorenzetti when he came to devise his own personification of that virtue.

The Sienese allegory contains considerable evidence of this debt. Its largest figure is that of the ruler, seated on a throne, the wings of which extend left and right to accommodate six slightly smaller seated female figures. Above this group, at the top of the wall, hover Faith, Hope, and Charity. To their left, and at the same height and scale, they are balanced by the single, winged figure of Sapientia, or Wisdom, a visual reference to the relationship between divine and natural law as stressed by Thomas Aquinas.[8] Wisdom is poised directly above the figure of Justice. This seventh cardinal virtue is on the same level as the other six, but her individual throne is placed further along the platform, to the left of the main group. This distinction between Justice and her sister virtues is no accident. Indeed, the inscription below draws attention to her as the starting point of the allegory:

[8] "Remota divinae sapientiae moventis omnia ad debitum finem obtinet rationem legis." This and other passages from Aquinas are quoted by Nicolai Rubenstein, "Political Ideas in Sienese Art: the Frescoes by Ambrogio Lorenzetti and Tadeo di Bartolo in the Palazzo Pubblico," *Journal of the Warburg and Courtauld Institutes* 21 (1958): 179–207. See also L. Zdekauer, "Iustitia, Immagine e Idea," *Bulletino senese di storia patria* 20 (1913): 384–425. For Ambrogio Lorenzetti, see George Rowley, *Ambrogio Lorenzetti*, 2 vols. (Princeton: Princeton University Press, 1958).

"Wherever this saintly virtue reigns, she induces unity among many souls, and these when gathered together, undertake a common good."[9]

It is possible that the isolation of Justice given visible expression by the painter may be traced back to the political thought of Aristotle. In the fifth book of the *Ethics*, he writes, "Justice is often thought to be the best of the virtues . . . it is not a part of virtue, but co-extensive with it." Moreover, it was Aristotle in book two of the *Ethics* who distinguished between the distributive and commutative roles of justice—a distinction emphasized by both Giotto and Ambrogio Lorenzetti in their respective treatments of the subject. The scales of Lorenzetti's Justice, for instance, hang from Wisdom above. Her winged agents, brandishing rod and sword, are labelled clearly as "Distributiva" and "Commutativa."

The inscriptions beneath the allegory draw attention to the cords of Justice. From her left and right, from her distributive and her commutative roles, they pass downwards to where they are joined together in the hands of Concord. She is a placid figure seated beneath Justice, her function underlined by the wooden smoothing plane she holds in her lap—an original and highly practical symbol. From her hands, the single united cord passes through the hands of twenty-four citizens, a significant number corresponding to the size of the Sienese general council at the time. These men stand on the lowest level of the fresco, nearest to the spectator and at the feet of the dominant personification of Good Government. Both for the painter and for his political advisors, this central figure must have posed a particularly sensitive problem. Power in the city resided in an inner council of nine elected magistrates, who served two-month terms of office. For ceremonial and certain judicial functions the Sienese, like many Italian city-states, employed the services of a *podestà*, a "foreigner" of some distinction who was invited to hold office for a limited time and with important circumscriptions of power. The Sienese statutes of 1262 were designed in part to protect civil liberties from the dangers of tyranny posed by individual rule—which must have been an important consideration, for both patron and painter, when the question of the personification of authority arose. That in itself may explain the exaggerated scale of the figure with its impassive, expressionless face. It is unmistakably human in form, and yet oversized in scale and devoid of personal characteristics.

Fortunately, Lorenzetti had one important visual precedent for the figure of Good Government. According to Vasari, Giotto painted "in the great Hall of the Podestà at Florence . . . a representation of the commune

---

[9] The Italian text of the inscription reads as follows:

> Questa santa virtù ladove regge
> induce ad unità li animi molti,
> e questi acciò ricolti,
> un ben comun per lo signor si fanno

The English translation given in text is my own.

plundered by many. The figure is represented as a judge, seated and with a sceptre in his hand, over whose head are the scales equally poised to indicate the measures meted out by him, while he is assisted by four virtues . . ."[10] The fresco does not survive, but what is almost certainly a direct reflection of it does: Vasari was incorrect in attributing to Giotto the fourteenth-century tomb of Bishop Tarlati of Arezzo, although among its relief sculptures, one, a representation of "il commune pelato," answers the description of the lost prototype.[11]

Evidence that Ambrogio Lorenzetti succeeded in providing a medieval commune with an impersonal symbol of its own authority survives in the form of a painted book cover, one of the official ledgers of the city containing accounts for the year 1344: on it the *Buongoverno* is depicted[12] (Figure F). This also serves to correct the wrongly restored initials above the figure's head in the allegorical fresco; the book cover shows that originally they read, predictably enough, C. S. C. V. To complete the civic symbolism of the figure, he is clothed in the black and white of the Sienese *balzana*, while at his feet the she-wolf suckles Romulus and Remus. Not to be outdone by the city of Rome, Siena claimed a parallel descent from the sons of Remus.

This last image reminds us of the increasing references in the late Middle Ages to antiquity.[13] Similarly, the figure of Pax provides an obvious visual link with the classical past. Her significance within the overall scheme of the allegory has always been recognized; in fact, shortly after the frescoes were painted, the room was named the "Sala della Pace" after this important virtue. Reclining as she does at the left end of the virtues' throne, olive branch in hand, she actually occupies the center of the entire fresco, both vertically and horizontally. The diaphanous draperies with which her recumbent form is clad reveal the anatomy of the figure beneath: breasts, torso, and navel. For comparable detail, as well as for the river-god pose of the figure, Ambrogio Lorenzetti must have referred to Graeco-Roman sculpture. That he did so from time to time is described, conveniently, by no less an authority than the fifteenth-century Florentine sculptor, Lorenzo Ghiberti. In his *Comentarii* he recounts an anecdote which tells us a great deal not only about Lorenzetti's antiquarian interests in the classical period, but also about the ambivalence with which that period was often treated in the late Middle Ages. Ghiberti refers to a statue of Venus, attributed to Lysippus, which was known to him only from a drawing by Lorenzetti. Apparently for a

[10] Giorgio Vasari, *The Lives of the Painters, Sculptors and Architects*, trans. A. B. Hinds (London: J. M. Dent & Sons, 1927), 1: 80–81.

[11] See Salamone Morpurgo, "Bruto, 'il buon giudice,' nell' Udienza dell' Arte della Lana in Firenze," *Miscellanea di storia dell' arte in onore di Igino Benvenuto Supino* (Florence: Olschki, 1933), pp. 141–63.

[12] Enzo Carli, *Le Tavoletti di Bicherna e di altri uffici dello stato di Siena* (Florence: Electa, 1950), 26: plates 1 and 15.

[13] H. Wieruszowski, "Art and the Commune in the Time of Dante," *Speculum* 19 (1944): 14–33.

time after its discovery this statue had occupied a place of honor on the Fonte
Gaia, in the center of the city. At a moment when Siena's fortunes were
waning, however, the citizens were persuaded that their reverence for the
pagan idol had offended the Virgin. Therefore they smashed it into small
pieces, which they proceeded to bury in Florentine soil, in the hope that
their ill fortune might be transferred to their old rivals.[14]

The figure of Peace once again demonstrates the painter's sympathy for
the policies and ideals of his civic patrons. The inscriptions beneath the
Buongoverno explains its purpose: "For this [Peace] without wars there
follows every civil result useful, necessary and pleasurable."[15] Peace was not
only desirable, it was increasingly emphasized by political writers of the late
thirteenth and early fourteenth centuries as the true end of civil government. When Dante stressed the importance of peace to human fulfillment in
his *De Monarchia* (c. 1312), he was contributing a body of literature which
stretched back to St. Augustine (although with a careful sidestepping of
Augustine's diatribe against Rome). By the early fourteenth century, however, the issue was a political one, focused on the plenitude of papal authority. As a contribution to the antipapal side of that debate, Marsilius of
Padua produced his treatise *De Pacis:*

> The city, according to Aristotle in the *Politics,* is the perfect community,
> having the full limit of self-sufficiency, which came into existence for the
> sake of living, but exists for the sake of living well. This . . . signifies the
> perfect, final cause of the city since those who live a civil life not only
> live, which beasts or slaves do too, but live well, having leisure for those
> liberal functions in which are exercised the virtues of both the practical
> and theoretic soul.[16]

The translation into Latin of Aristotle's *Politics* around 1260 was only one
factor in the growth and secularization of political thought in the period.
What is of particular interest to the art historian is the fact that the use of
classical sources by writers in the early fourteenth century finds a parallel in
the visual arts as well. Antiquity holds the key to a new iconography.

From the allegory of Good Government we now turn briefly to the
frescoes which illustrate its effects upon town and countryside (Figure G).

[14] For the original text of Ghiberti's *Commentarii,* together with full notes, see Julius von
Schlosser, *Lorenzo Ghibertis Denkwordigkeiten,* 2 vols. (Berlin: J. Band, 1912).

[15] The Italian text of the inscription reads as follows:

> per questo, senza guerre,
> seguita poi ogni civile effetto
> utile necessario e di diletto

The English translation given in text is my own.

[16] Cited by Alan Gewirth, *Marsilius of Padua, The Defender of Peace* (New York: Columbia University Press, 1951), p. 64. See also pp. 3–31. For further consideration of the
subject, see Alexander Passerin d'Entrêves, *The Medieval Contribution to Political
Thought* (London: Oxford University Press, 1939).

Here the advantages of peace are described with an eye for detail which has earned for these paintings their deserved reputation as one of the finest examples of descriptive art in western Europe. The painted city bears an obvious relation to the medieval town in which Lorenzetti himself worked. On the other hand, we must be careful not to miss the symbolism with which this deceptively straightforward cityscape is invested. Merchants, builders, and tradesmen in the painting provide the social historian with a wealth of information about local practices, tools, and techniques; they also appear as representatives of the labors. Other figures have purely symbolic value. Like Giotto, Lorenzetti uses the device of a group of dancers to express harmony (Figure H). And lest we are tempted to question the actual possibility of such public displays, it is worth recalling that dancing in the streets was expressly forbidden by the statutes of 1262.

The peaceful countryside is similarly subtle in its combination of traditional symbolism and a startling naturalism. For such a loving description of the Tuscan landscape there are simply no pictorial rivals in the period. The analogy is rather with those poets of the early fourteenth century who awoke to the sights, sounds, and smells of the open air. Folgore da San Gimignano (d. 1317) was one of these, with his evocations of "la gentil campagna/tutta fiorita di bell' erba fresca." His poem on the month of June might almost be a description of Lorenzetti's extensive panorama, with his charming celebration of hills and trees, villas and castles, all seen within the embrace of civic life:

> Di giugno dovè una montagnetta
> coverta di bellissimi arborscelli
> con trenta ville e dodici castelli
> che siano entorno ad una cittadetta.[17]

It is worth remembering, however, that Folgore wrote his poems as a sequence on the twelve months. A careful look at the painted landscape reveals that among the workers in the fields all twelve of the labors of the months are represented. For all their apparent realism, they are no less symbolic than the four seasons represented by conventional figures painted into the borders of the fresco.

In conclusion, we have seen that Ambrogio Lorenzetti's frescoes of Good and Bad Government reveal a program as complete (and in many ways as theologically orthodox) as that of a twelfth-century cathedral facade. Their message is an extension of what is expressed in Duccio's *Maestà*, but in place of the conventional iconography of Christian devotion situated within the

[17] For full text and translation, see Folgore da San Gimignano, *The Months of the Year; twelve sonnets,* with translation by T. C. Chubb (Sanbornville, N.H.: Wake-Brook House, 1960).

confines of a church, the frescoes introduce innovative imagery designed specifically for a secular building. The paintings deal directly with the relationship between spiritual and temporal power, and in so doing reveal the ability of the visual artist to give pictorial form to one of the most important intellectual issues of the time. In his combination of old and new, in his careful orthodoxy and daring originality, Ambrogio Lorenzetti was not unworthy of the age of Thomas Aquinas and Dante Alighieri.

1. Figure A Duccio di Buoninsegna
   "Maestà" Altarpiece
   1308–11
   Museo dell' Opera del Duomo, Siena

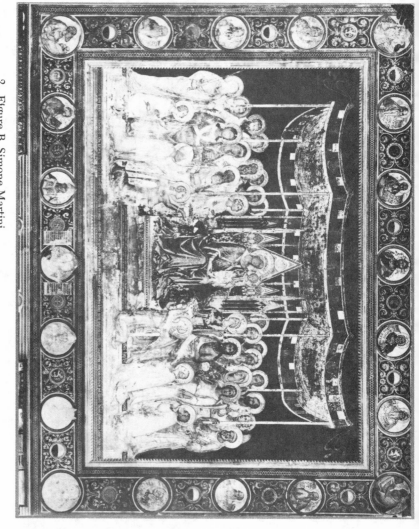

2. Figure B Simone Martini
   "Madonna Enthroned with the Child, Angels, and
   Saints"
   1315, retouched 1321
   Palazzo Pubblico, Siena

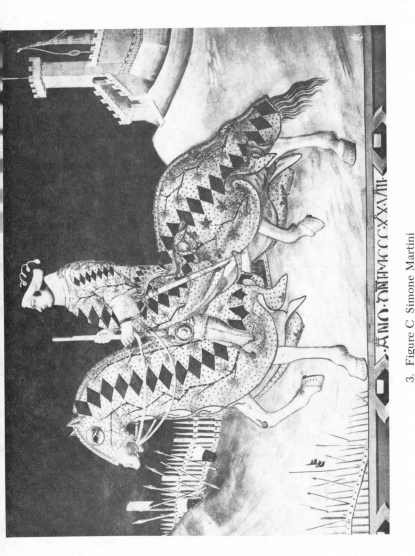

3. Figure C Simone Martini
"Equestrian Portrait of Guidoriccio da
Foligno" (detail)
1328
Palazzo Pubblico, Siena

4. Figure D Ambrogio Lorenzetti
"Allegory of Good Government"
1337–39
Palazzo Pubblico, Sienna

5. Figure E Ambrogio Lorenzetti
"Allegory of Bad Government"
1337–39
Palazzo Pubblico, Siena

6. Figure F Painted Book Cover of a Biccherna (Official City Ledger)
1344
Archivo di Stato, Siena

7. Figure G   Ambrogio Lorenzetti
"Effects of Good Government on the Countryside"
(detail)
1337–39
Palazzo Pubblico, Siena

8. Figure H Ambrogio Lorenzetti
   "Effects of Good Government on the City" (detail)
   1337–39
   Palazzo Pubblico, Siena

8

Exiles in the Earthly City: The Heritage of Saint Augustine

JAMES DOUGHERTY
University of Notre Dame

I. Classical and Christian Precedents*

"There are two commonwealths," wrote a Roman man of letters, seeking a metaphor to describe our moral and spiritual responsibilities. In this case the writer was not Saint Augustine, but Seneca, the pagan dramatist and philosopher. Born a Spaniard and a Roman citizen, he described all people as having dual citizenship.

> There are two commonwealths—the one, a vast and truly common state, which embraces alike gods and men, in which we look neither to this corner of earth nor to that, but measure our city's bounds by the path of the sun; the other, the one to which we have been assigned by the accident of birth. This will be the commonwealth of the Athenians or of the Carthaginians, or of any other city that belongs, not to all, but to some particular race of men. (*On Leisure*, 4.1)[1]

This formulation allows Seneca, as a Stoic, to express his sense of both the proximate and the ultimate duties of humanity. While the universal commonwealth may be the "higher," ordinarily a human being does not have to choose between them. "Both. . . and" is the formula for Seneca's vision of the ethical life: one city contained within another.

The early Christians, living in the less expansive latitudes of Seneca's universal city, phrased citizenship more disjunctively. Doubtless because it often applied to their actual situation, Christians quickly took up the scriptural image of God's faithful as a community of exiles within a foreign and unsympathetic city. Their imagery of exile was also grounded in the contem-

---

*Some of the ideas in this essay originated in an early version of my book *The Fivesquare City* (University of Notre Dame Press, 1980). Parts of this first section appear, in slightly different form and context, in the first two chapters of that book.

[1] Seneca, *Moral Essays*, trans. John W. Basore (New York: G. P. Putnam's Sons, 1932), 2:187–89. Basore translates *terminos civitatis nostrae* as "bounds of our citizenship."

porary reality of the Roman empire. Whereas the ancient world determined citizenship by one's ancestral city, the conquests of Rome, destroying the political autonomy of the Mediterranean cities, left their populations in a semi-stateless condition where only Roman citizenship—inherited or acquired—was of value. One was part of the Roman *imperium*, enjoying its protection, or one was nothing. The early church often made the resolution of these anxieties its symbol: "Once you were not a people at all," Saint Peter writes to an audience of Jewish converts "living among foreigners" throughout Asia Minor; "and now you are the People of God" (1 Peter 2.10).[2] "You are no longer aliens or foreign visitors," Saint Paul tells the gentile converts at Ephesus; "you are citizens like all the saints" (Eph. 2.19). That is, they had found a new citizenship in the city of God, a city inaccessible to the state-killing expansionism of the Roman *imperium* and yet present, as a "church," within the gates of Ephesus or the towns of Cappadocia.

Thus the image of exile in Babylon both conferred citizenship and took it away: assuming citizenship in the heavenly Jerusalem, the Christians became, in the cities where they lived, "visitors and pilgrims" (1 Peter 2.11). They were not hostile aliens, neither treasonous nor subversive, but men and women with only a limited interest in the cities where they lived. The city of God had a prior claim to their services, as Syracuse might on a Syracusan residing in Corinth.[3] The first parable of the *Shepherd of Hermas* expounds Christian detachment in the imagery of a resident alien's contingent legal status:

> You know that you servants of God are living in a foreign country, for your city is far from this city. Now, if you know the city in which you are eventually to dwell, why do you secure fields, rich establishments, houses, and superfluous dwellings? The person who secures such things for this city does not think of returning to his own city. Foolish, miserable man of divided purpose, do you not realize that these superfluities belong to somebody else and are in the control of another? For the lord of this city will say: "I do not wish you to reside in my city. Go out of it, for you do not live according to my laws. . . ." What are you going to do, then, since you are subject to the law of your own city? . . . Be prepared, so that, when the ruler of this city wishes to expel you for resisting his law, you may come out of his city and enter your own and there rejoice . . . in the observance of your own proper law.[4]

The reciprocal of such contingency is the indifference of aliens to the fate of their temporary residence. Sustained by its vision of a heavenly city, the

---

[2] *The Jerusalem Bible*, ed. Alexander Jones (New York: Doubleday, 1966).

[3] A. H. M. Jones, *The Decline of the Ancient World* (New York: Holt Rinehart & Winston, 1966), p. 237.

[4] *The Apostolic Fathers*, trans. Francis X. Glimm, et. al. (New York: Cima Publishing Co., Inc., 1947), pp. 286–87 (1–3, 5–6). The translation of the second verse has been slightly altered.

book of Revelation recites with equanimity—even with relish—its lurid account of secular agony, conflagration and massacre, the travail and ruin of an empire, in which Christians must suffer quite as much as Caesar-worshippers. Marked with the royal seal of God's kingdom, they wait passively for an envoy of that kingdom to summon them out of the great city's final throes and set them on the road to their own city—as once Cyrus had set the Israelites on the way to Jerusalem after his conquest of Babylon.

The City of God is structured on a colossal magnification of the last five chapters of the Apocalpyse.[5] Augustine begins with Alaric's sack of Rome. Whether protected in their sanctuaries or sharing the city's fate in death or captivity, as many did, Christian Romans accept the rapine as a judgment of God, purifying his faithful and punishing the impious pagans. Their stake in the city is not absolute. Their allegiance is not to Rome, but rather to a *civitas peregrina*, a community of sojourners. *Peregrinus* is the Roman legal term for a resident alien. His civic duty, Cicero had written, was simply not to meddle in the affairs of his host country.[6] Augustine describes the Christian as a spiritual *peregrinus*, whose membership in the city of God limits his involvement in the earthly city.

"Earthly city," *civitas terrena*, is in Augustine an irresolvably ambiguous term. Figuratively it is the realm of exclusively immediate concerns, the city of self and self-sufficiency; to such a city the Christian must be only a stranger. Literally, however, it is the place of one's mortal life, one's human loyalties. *The City of God* does not summon Christians to dereliction of their duties as human beings. Since the life of the saints is to be a communal life (19.5), the image of the *civitas peregrina* suggests the cohesiveness and sense of mutual support which a group of resident aliens might develop within their host city. Furthermore, this social responsibility is interlocked with the concerns of the larger community in which they live: "Since our mortal state is the same for all, there ought to be common cause between the two cities in what concerns that life" (19.17). Since its own well-being is fostered by peace among its diverse membership and peace with nonmembers too, the city of God "makes use of" the peace—such as it is—provided by the civil state, and "seeks and fosters an alliance of human beings in regard to all that concerns the mortal nature of men." Augustine devotes book nineteen to demonstrating that the virtues of Christianity—charity, justice, the pursuit of peace— are exactly those that promote the common weal of all the earthly city. Peace,

---

[5] Augustine, *The City of God*, trans. Gerald G. Walsh, et. al. (New York: Fathers of the Church, Inc., 1950–54). Translations have been amended sometimes to make a point more forcefully. In addition, the conventional phrase, "the city of man," has been replaced with inclusive language throughout, except where it appears in untranslated quotations. Augustine's own phrase, *civitas terrena*, "earthly city," is not "gender exclusive" in any case.

[6] Cicero, *De Officiis*, trans. Walter Miller (Cambridge: Harvard University Press, 1938), p. 127 (1.34.125).

he says, depends on the harmonious order of diverse beings, and harmony among mortals depends on their recognition and pursuit of a common goal. Therefore Christians' common dedication to the heavenly city should not only bind them together as a community, but provide a basis for civil agreement on the nature of such virtues as justice, humility, and mercy, which might foster the peace of the earthly city though they are pursued for the sake of the heavenly (19.23–27).

Nevertheless, Augustine cannot describe Christians with the dual-citizenship image used by Seneca; they are *not* citizens of the earthly city, however they may make common cause with it. For him citizenship still carried its age-old implications of spiritual allegiance and of religious cult. Therefore his recognition of humanity's common cause is always linked with a qualification: "so long as matters of faith and worship are not involved." He usually suggests a restrained and passive presence for Christians in the earthly city:

> So long as her life in the earthly city is that of a captive and an alien. . .
> [the heavenly city] has no hesitation about keeping in step with the civil
> law which governs matters pertaining to the sustenance of mortal life.
> (19.17)

Christians *use* the civil peace and *comply* with state authority. They do not build the city, they do not reform its laws, they do not meddle in the public affairs of their host country. Their minds focused on a city outside of time, they perceive the timebound or secular city differently from those for whom it is the only reality. For them, this city is only "the way"; and in Augustine's mind, the heavenly city does not incorporate the way and make it holy. He does not believe that a Christian soul, sheltered by God, may make a home in this world. His grammar is not "both . . . and," but "either . . . or," reflecting his recognition that the goals of human comfort and physical sufficiency cannot be achieved without a wholeminded absorption which precludes devotion to God. Augustine was convinced that the short-term goods of this life could not be attained without a commitment to attaining them which amounted to a religious conviction. And these goods would cause the one who gained them to lose sight of God's absolute kingship over the world and worship instead the human *civitas* which brought these blessings. A measure of this Augustinian detachment is the allegorical mode of the book itself: the culture, life, and history of human communities enter his account only insofar as they serve as the ground for "spiritual" interpretations; in themselves, earthly cities are only shadows flickering in the corridor of history.

This patristic image of the religious life, as the way of an exiled people travelling to a far-off city, has been perennially invoked by Christians. The iconography of pilgrimage and crusade are embedded in church institutions and church architecture. The traditional architectural forms of the Western church are, as the critic Rudolph Schwarz once wrote, "way-form."[7] Towered and crenellated, the Gothic cathedral rises before the pilgrim in the image of the heavenly city; and, once inside, the visitor's eye is still led onward toward the city of light. Saint Mary Major and the Basilica of Saint Peter loom at the termini of processionary ways carved through secular Rome. Even that mortally stationary institution of the Christian Church, the parish, owes its name to the Greek word for "wayfarer."

Likewise the religious spirit in Western literature has frequently taken a wayfaring mode. The structure of Torquato Tasso's *Jerusalem Delivered* rests on the crusaders' painful advance to, and conquest of, the holy city. Dante journeys through the city of Dis toward that vision of peace which surmounts the summit of the earthly paradise. The refugee people in Luther's hymn, fleeing toward God's fortress city, abandon to the prince of this world all worldly things—"body, goods, honor, child and wife"—and count them little loss in comparison with the kingdom into which they are coming. The drama of *The Pilgrim's Progress* depends on our knowledge that Christian must extricate himself from every situation he encounters, whether pleasant or grim, because he is on the way to the Celestial City.

At the same time, it has not been easy to sustain that anagogical imagination in which reality is perceived as the way, and referred to a far-off Jerusalem. The way becomes sufficient reality itself. One might consider the fate of the heavenly city in those works of English literature where it serves as a pilgrim's goal. The city retreats beyond the vanishing point: poems ostensibly aiming for "Jerusalem" as goal lose their way, like their heroes, in an endless advance through that dark forest which has so long obsessed the Northern imagination, a spiritual wilderness full of monsters, witches, and ungodly men and women. The medieval poem *The Pearl* culminates in a vision of the heavenly city, but it lies across a river from the hero; and the touch of the water awakens him from his dream. In *Piers Plowman* the poet loses track of his journey motif, takes up other allegorical devices, and at last abandons the poem. Chaucer's pilgrims never reach Canterbury: their wayward storytelling occupies as much of the poem as he was able to complete. Spenser's Arthurian knights ride out on quests which both test the virtues they represent and also bring them eventually to the heavenly city—or at least to Cleopolis, its earthly counterpart. But the poem becomes an unceasing march through the forest, an interminable series of adventures and battles with the forces of the adversary, where castles and cities are more likely to prove deceptions than true comforts. Spenser abandons the poem before any of his knights have reached their goal. John Bunyan's dreamer sees Christian received into the celestial city, but then himself awakens, with ominous circularity, back in his den in the wilderness of this world. Since

---

[7] Rudolph Schwarz, *The Church Incarnate*, trans. Cynthia Harris (Chicago: Henry Regnery Co., 1958), p. 135.

then the city has waned into the goal of secular pilgrims like Benjamin Franklin and the heroes of Charles Dickens, Scott Fitzgerald, and Thomas Wolfe, who usually find that what seemed the Celestial City proves in fact Vanity Fair, and that from the gates of Jerusalem there is a short plunge to the City of Destruction. In the poetry of William Carlos Williams and T. S. Eliot, the shining, far-off city proves only a mirage, "more than a little false" to Williams, "unreal" to Eliot.

II. W. H. Auden's City of the Flesh

Another modern social poet, W. H. Auden, often expressed his dissatisfaction with a culture obsessed with images of endless struggle in the wilderness. "We live," he said in 1950, "in a new age . . . in which the heroic image is not the nomad wandering through the desert or over the ocean, but the less exciting figure of the builder, who renews the ruined walls of the city."[8] Auden's imagery here, of course, is that of Isaiah and Nehemiah, of the return from Babylon. Auden wished to replace Isaiah's apocalyptic vision with the prosaic, compromised struggles of Nehemiah; to discredit the romantic outcasts of Melville and Rimbaud in favor of a communally minded imagination. (Nathan Scott has called it the poetry of civic virtue.[9]) Auden's is not a millennial city, but a manifold symbol of human life in time.

Like Augustine's, Auden's earthly city is not vision of peace: his early poems describe its paralyzed machinery and impotent leadership; in mid-career he writes of "unhappy" and "starving" cities; his late poem "City Without Walls" leads us into a metropolis whose "Asphalt Lands are lawless marches / where gangs clash and cops turn / robber-barons."[10] Auden's response to this reality, however, is not Augustine's. He does not measure the inadequacy of its justice against some transcendent ideal, nor does he propose a search for a perfect *civitas*, either in this world or in another. (In a 1938 poem it is the Nazis who say, "We build the Perfect City time shall never alter."[11])

A city in time, Auden's Just City adopts imperfect means to effect an imperfect peace. We cannot do more; we may not do less. In his ballad "As I

[8] W. H. Auden, *The Enchafèd Flood; or, The Romantic Iconography of the Sea* (New York: Random House, 1950), p. 53.

[9] Nathan Scott, *The Poetry of Civic Virtue* (Philadelphia: Fortress Press, 1976). Chapter 3 is devoted to Auden.

[10] Auden's early poems: see "Consider this and in your time" and "Get there if you can and see the land you once were proud to own"; middle poems: see "Hearing of harvests rotting in the valleys"—all in *The English Auden*, ed. Edward Mendelson (New York: Random House, 1977). *City Without Walls and Other Poems* (New York: Random House, 1971).

[11] W. H. Auden, "Commentary" from *In Time of War*, in *The English Auden*, p. 266. For a discussion of Auden's lifelong absorption with this city image, see Monroe K. Spears, *Dionysus and the City* (New York: Oxford University Press, 1970), pp. 82–90.

Walked Out One Evening," he hears in the city's chiming clocks a lesson in mutability, which concludes "You shall love your crooked neighbour / With your crooked heart."[12] The crookedness is a condition of the love. In this city, the bond of community is the mutual, tolerant recognition of fallibility and possible bad faith. Anden's view of the human community, after 1939, was influenced by his contacts with the British theologian Charles Williams, who propounded a view of the *civitas* as a structure for bearing one another's burdens: a "co-inherence" based on our acknowledgment of our own weakness and that of our neighbor.[13] Here Auden and Williams return to an Augustinian principle: all who dwell in the earthly city share in the franchise of mortality. In his poem "Memorial for the City" (1949), which is dedicated to Williams, Auden develops a political and psychological allegory upon the image of a double city—not two cities, but one city divided against itself.[14] Like Augustine, he begins with a historical fact, the ruin of Europe immediately after World War II. Against the ruins of Leningrad, Warsaw, Berlin and Vienna, and a Europe newly divided east and west, Auden sets a vision of the city as a symbol of human union, of the harmonizing of contraries. In exegetical terms: his anagogical city of human concord is both an allegorical city where sacred and secular motives are reconciled, and also a moral city in which spirit and flesh support and temper each other in the individual psyche.

In the first part of his poem Auden argues, as Augustine had, that the Christian view of time delivers humankind from the meaninglessness of purely profane history. But soon he parts company with Augustine, saying that the secular world is not impoverished by the rise of this "New [heavenly] City." He sketches a figural history of Europe in which secular acts take their share in the great typological argument which history embodies: "the acts of the City," he writes, "bore a double meaning." The interregnum between Christ's ascension and his second coming is here not a period of trial and delay while the saints wait passively for their deliverance. The sacramentalizing of the temporal can put us at peace with our world, opening everything to the religious imagination. "Building the city" is not Babylonian arrogance, but a process of devotion and charity; it is not done once for all, in a gesture of architectural or social imperialism, but again and again, renewing the communal bonds between human beings.

This ideal, he writes, was destroyed by the Reformation, which threw between secular and sacred a "gap / No rite could cross," fostering not a secular city but a profane city, a private rather than a public conscience. In his view, World War II is the outcome of that division. Not just Coventry and Tokyo have been torn apart, but the City itself. Of the barbed wire that in 1949 divided Europe and its cities, he writes:

12 *The English Auden*, p. 228.
13 Charles Williams, "The Redeemed City," *The Image of the City and Other Essays* (London: Oxford University Press, 1958), pp. 102–10.
14 W. H. Auden, *Nones* (New York: Random House, 1951), pp. 39–44.

> where it likes a place, a path, a railroad ends,
> The humor, the cuisine, the rites, the taste,
> The pattern of the City, are erased.

The pattern which war destroys is not just the *urbs*, the physical city, but the *civitas*, that is, its culture, manners, tolerance of diversity, and climate of civilized discussion. Inclusive rather than exclusive, these are the constituents of secular justice, the incorporating tissues of the just city.

Then Auden transforms his image of the divided city into a psychological trope.[15] "Across our sleep," he continues, "The barbed wire also runs": the fundamental tragedy of our time is the denial of the flesh. Not Augustinian flesh, the self's lust for domination, but what Augustine called *mortalitas*, human weakness and fallibility, the common bond of all who dwell in the *civitas terrena*. Auden's 'flesh' is *soma*, rock-bottom physical process and psychical energy, the despair of ideologues (whether religious or worldly) and the hope of the race:

> for It the wire and the ruins are not the end:
> This is the flesh we are but never would believe,
>   . . . This is Adam waiting for His City.

The denial of the flesh in social and political life has sent humanity in pursuit of the perfect city, a utopian or totalitarian dream, rather than the just city. In personal life, the denial has caused the sane city to degenerate into the conscious city, that mental projection of Whitman, Baudelaire, and Joyce. Auden believes that to recognize and re-enfranchise the flesh might temper the hubris of the autocratic spirit and save mankind, by renewing the just and sane City in place of "Metropolis, that too-great city," whose deluded assumption of human perfectibility has proved man's ruin.

Almost contemporary with "Memorial for the City," Auden wrote *Horae Canonicae*, a set of meditations on the canonical hours of prayer.[16] These explicitly urban poems deepen and complicate our view of the just city and the harmony of spirit and flesh. The sequence begins with Matins, when the citizen assumes his "historical share of care / For a lying self-made city," and devotes himself, through his work, to one of the ideals which the human spirit has defined: he becomes "an incarnation of *Fortitudo, Justitia, Nous*." Of these ideals Auden says, "we owe them / basilicas, divas, / dictionaries, pastoral verse, / the courtesies of the city." Without dedication to such ideals, we would be "still / wandering through forests without / a consonant to our names, / . . . lacking / all notion of a city."

---

[15] Auden's use of urban imagery for the psychological life, implicit in his poetry in the 1930s, surfaces in *New Year Letter* (London: Faber and Faber, 1941), which speaks of the music of Buxtehude as "a civitas of sound"; of "the polis of our friends"; and of making a city "from the muddled heart."

[16] W. H. Auden, *Collected Shorter Poems 1927–1957* (New York: Random House, 1967), pp. 323–38.

But the counterfoil of this dedication is renunciation—renunciation of the sloth and appetite of the flesh, in the name of the ideals of the spirit. In order to bear the burdens of the flesh, the city must sacrifice the flesh! The price of the city is a blood price. Auden leads us from the fates of Abel and of Remus, to the major theme of Sext and Nones: the crucifixion of the Word made flesh, victim of the city's lust for power. In the Vespers poem, two citizens argue over the nature of the *civitas*, a "utopian" urging the triumph of spirit and will, an "arcadian" yearning for comfort and play. The two can be reconciled, Auden says, only if both "remember our victim": only the Crucified One can heal the breach of spirit and flesh, assuring that the "secular wall will safely stand."

This prototypical day ends in the dawn-song of Lauds—not entering a heavenly city, but praying God's blessing on a harmonized secular world of nature, persons, and society:

> Bright shines the sun on creatures mortal;
> Men of their neighbours become sensible;
> . . . .
> Men of their neighbours become sensible;
> God bless the Realm, God bless the People.

Thus, to advocate a worldview in which secular and sacred are joined, Auden's poems enact that world, discovering within the earthly city a multiplex spiritual allegory. This allegory, however, never makes light of the actual, physical cities upon which it is founded. For it discovers the city's business to be the collaborative support of our human frailty: the powerless, the creaturely, the physical, the mortal. To build this city is a secular (but not profane) version of that building up of a communal structure into which Saint Paul welcomed, as citizens, the "aliens and foreign visitors" who were the church at Ephesus (Eph. 2.20–22).

III. The Walled Cities of Camus

In that same postwar decade, an Algerian Frenchman thought also of human justice, divided cities, and the sacrifice of the innocent. For Albert Camus the image of the earthly city was even more important than it was for W. H. Auden. "There are no more deserts," he wrote in 1939; "there are no more islands." Rejecting as Auden did the solitude of the nomad, he said, "There remain great cities."[17] Though his short fiction often wanders to the desert or the jungle, his novels make their home in the city. But through that city Camus, again like Auden, traces the fissure of divided consciousness.

In his novels and travel sketches the vision recurs of a sensual, pagan city—Algiers, Cadiz, Oran—where on flowered terraces above a sunstruck

[17] Albert Camus, "Le Minotaure: ou La Halte d'Oran," *Essais* (Paris: Gallimard, 1965), p. 813.

bay humankind still enjoys a prelapsarian unity of being.[18] The vision fosters
no sense of history or of remorse; it defies detachment; it preserves a city
artlessly profane. But even the early travel sketches recognize that this is a
fugitive vision. One's homeland," he confesses, "is always recognized at the
moment of losing it."[19] The city's image in Camus is fragmented by themes
of death and exile, diffracted by the lens of allegory.

In *The Stranger* (1942) a shadow of death falls between the sensual man
and his sensual city. Sentenced to die for killing an Arab, Meursault discovers the beauty of Algiers only as it is lost to him. He recognizes at last a
confraternity with the world—not as his home, but as the image of his own
alienation: "One and the same fate was bound to fall not only on me but on
thousands of millions. . . . All alike would be condemned to die one day."[20]
The play *State of Siege* (1948) uses a walled city, Cadiz, to represent how we
are cut off from life and love by the powers of death; that is, by ideologies of
guilt and by systems of justice that are based on the power to inflict death.
The play's hero, Diego, forswears his pleasure in the city, to struggle against
injustice and oppression. In Camus, as in Auden, the city-builder must
renounce the flesh.

We are cut off as well from direct and simple perception of the city.
Camus casts before his city a grid of allegorical implication, so that it must be
taken no longer for what it seems but rather for what it means. In *State of
Siege, The Plague* (1947), *The Rebel* (1951), and *The Fall* (1956), the city is not
the simple reality that it was in the travel sketches and in *The Stranger*. It
becomes the key figure for Camus's secular humanism, representing the
single soul, the human community, and our human metaphysical situation.
In losing the profane city, Camus discovers the *civitas terrena*.[21]

Through *The Rebel* this image of the city moves as a minor but significant thread. Early in the book he quotes Epicurus: "Against death all of us
mortals alike dwell in an unfortified city."[22] Developing this metaphor,
Camus says that the Greek philosopher's banishment of the gods was a
sealing-off of this city, a declaration that "all the unhappiness of human
beings springs from the hope that tempts them from the silence of the citadel
and exposes them on the ramparts in expectation of salvation." For Lucretius, "the closed citadel becomes a fortified camp. *Moenia mundi*, the

[18] Albert Camus, "L'Été à Alger," *Essais*, p. 75.
[19] Written before Camus had gone across the sea, this essay expresses a spiritual rather
than a physical alienation.
[20] Albert Camus, *The Stranger*, trans. Stuart Gilbert (New York: Vintage, 1957), p. 152.
Here, and in the translations used later, I have made minor adjustments of phrasing when
necessary.
[21] Camus wrote a thesis on Saint Augustine and Plotinus, for the *diplôme d'études
supérieures* at the University of Algiers. So his allegory of a walled city may be in debt not
only to traditional Western imagery, but also to one of the originators of that tradition.
[22] Vatican Sayings 31, in *Epicurus*, ed. Cyril Bailey (Oxford: Oxford University Press,
1926), pp. 110–11. Camus's translation reads, "une citadelle démantelée."

ramparts of the world, is one of the key expressions in Lucretius's rhetoric. The main preoccupation in this armed camp is, of course, to silence hope."[23] To hope is to imagine a condition different from what we now suffer. To silence hope is to banish from the mind the city afar, to wall the imagination within the world given by experience. In Camus's imagery, the earthly city is a colonial capital in revolt against *la métropole*.[24] Besieged by death and absurdity, his rebels await no deliverance, no envoy from another city. Christians, on the other hand, have accepted the resurrection and the kingdom as a sufficient answer to human suffering, and so have counseled earthly patience and passivity. Likewise the revolutionaries of the nineteenth and twentieth centuries used their dream of a just city to justify political expedience, terrorism, and recklessness with human life. Camus remains a man of hope, but his is a conditional hope, grounded on an imagination that refuses to relinquish its vivid grasp of the real. At the end of his essay he returns to his urban image to contrast all forms of millennarianism with his own humanistic "rebellion": "The men of Europe . . . forget the present for the future, the fate of humanity for the delusion of power, the misery of the slums for a radiant city,[25] ordinary justice for an empty promised land" (305). Camus urges upon his reader an ethos of exile. Like Augustine's, this exile implies a renunciation of self-seeking. Unlike Augustine's, though, it also renounces eschatological hope. There is now only one city; within its walls, humans must struggle out of their own private egotism toward a community founded on justice and compassion.

The Plague[26] develops most fully Camus's image of the walled earthly city. The Algerian city of Oran is under quarantine, closed up and put on its own resources to cope with an epidemic of bubonic plague. The novel's hero is Bernard Rieux, a doctor who devotes himself utterly to his city's well-being, tending the dying and seeking to stem the epidemic. The other characters all have their eyes set on some far-away city. The journalist Rambert is always seeking to escape from Oran, to return to Paris and his wife. The revolutionary Tarrou was once committed to building a secular Jerusalem. The Jesuit priest Paneloux, a scholar of Saint Augustine, confidently interprets the pestilence as God's apocalyptic challenge, punishing sinners and reminding men that they are pilgrims.

For these three—Rambert, Tarrou, and Paneloux—the novel is a con-

---

[23] Albert Camus, *The Rebel*, trans. Anthony Bower (New York: Vintage, 1956), pp. 28–30. Lucretius's phrase is from *De Rerum Natura*, 1.73.

[24] Camus's opposition to the colonial regime in Algeria probably informs his image of the self-sufficient human city. Or vice versa!

[25] Camus wrote "la misère des banlieues pour une cité radieuse," a phrase significantly midway between the New Jerusalem and Le Corbusier's mechanist utopia, *La Ville Radieuse*.

[26] Albert Camus, *The Plague*, trans. Stuart Gilbert (New York: The Modern Library, n.d.).

version story, since each eventually turns away from his visionary city to the
torment of Oran, and takes up sanitary or nursing work. Tarrou, repudiating
political homicide as a "plague," says that henceforth he will stand with the
victims and seek to become a healer. He says, "Once I'd definitely refused to
kill, I doomed myself to an exile that can never end." And he asks, "Can one
be a saint without believing in God?" (229f.). For him, fighting plague in
Oran is both an attack on death and a "saintly" renunciation of power over life
and death. Paneloux, chastened by the deaths of the innocent, tells the
people that

> we all were up against the rampart that plague had built around us, and
> in its lethal shadow we must work out our salvation. He, Father
> Paneloux, refused to have recourse to those easy solutions that would
> enable him to scale that wall. (201)

He renounces the eschatological view that made of suffering a transparent
allegory. And he takes up Camus's own figure of the enclosed city, making
common cause with Rieux against *mortalitas*. In place of the road to the New
Jerusalem, he sets up an image of the suffering and abandoned Christ.[27]

Whether visitors, like Rambert and Tarrou, or citizens, like Paneloux
and Rieux, all become "exiles." This term, first used to describe visitors
caught in the quarantine, is soon applied to all residents of Oran, and
eventually Camus extends it to the secular human condition:

> No longer were there individual destinies; only a collective destiny,
> made of plague and the emotions shared by all. Strongest of these
> emotions was the sense of exile and of deprivation. . . . Without memo-
> ries, without hope, they lived for the moment only. Indeed, the here
> and now had come to mean everything to them. (151, 165)

Camus's "exile" is in some respects like Augustine's *civitas peregrina*. All
egotistical satisfactions—all that lies outside the chosen city's boundaries—
must be renounced. And this new, higher citizenship replaces both the terror
and the glamour of free selfhood with the undiscriminating comradeship of
soldiers under siege. At the end, when the plague wanes and the quarantine
is lifted, the lovers like Rambert are liberated from their exile. But Rieux's
wife has died, and Tarrou and Paneloux both have perished. "For those
others who aspired beyond and above the human individual toward something they could not even imagine, there had been no answer" (271). Rieux
presents his own narrative as a kind of answer, for it is

> the record of what had had to be done, and what assuredly would have
> to be done again in the never ending fight against terror and its
> relentless onslaughts, despite their personal afflictions, by all who,

[27] Paneloux describes Christ as "experiencing agony in his body and in his soul" (202). In
The Rebel, Camus stressed that on the cross Christ experienced despair (32).

> while unable to be saints but refusing to bow down to pestilences, strive
> their utmost to be healers. (278)

This novel was begun during the Nazi occupation. Some of its details
suggest that it should be read as an allegorical account of the Resistance. But
the reader need not seek such an external reference. Inside the novel there
are more inclusive significances. One is proposed to Rieux by Tarrou: the
plague is injustice, including the taking of life in the name of a "higher"
justice; people must struggle against communicating or even tolerating this
plague. On this political level, the plague might someday retreat, exile might
end, and we might be restored to that profane city where we are fully at
home.[28] But on the metaphysical level created by the interaction of Rieux
and Paneloux, it does seem that the struggle and exile are everlasting, for
they refer to the victimization and suffering which human beings must
always endure, evade them how they may. Here the issue is not truly one of
justice, for to call *mortalitas* "injustice" is to imply an exterior standard by
which to measure it. The agnostic Camus cannot, like Job, ask for vindication
against the malfeasance of God.[29] Perhaps more appropriate terms for this
highest human virtue, terms which Rieux uses elsewhere, are compassion,
or sympathy, or love.

With the passage of years, the specific political allegories of *The Plague*
have grown less visible. Though the novel still appears dominated by its
ideas, Camus has not pulled reality out of shape (as he did in *State of Siege*),
in order to match it to his message. The novel is itself a proof of Camus's
conviction that experience has priority over ideology. Oran is certainly a
microcosm of the *civitas terrena;* but at the same time, Oran is unquestiona-
bly a city on the Algerian littoral, whose populace, weather, and boredom are
those Camus once described in a travel sketch. In dialogue with Tarrou or
Paneloux, Rieux may speak of his responsibility for "humanity"; but in the
narrative he is charged with concrete tasks to arrest the outbreak of plague in
Oran, and to minister to its victims. While refusing to mount the city's
ramparts and look for relief from a celestial city, Camus has nevertheless
constructed a story in which Seneca's universal commonwealth is made
manifest in the hospitals and restaurants of an actual city, in a specific corner
of the world, between the desert and the sea.

IV. The Recent Tradition: Redeeming Babylon

Auden and Camus put forth these re-visions of the earthly city in the
years that followed World War II. While the image had been thus secularized, it had not been profaned. In the decades that followed, religious

---

[28] In *The Rebel*, Camus wrote, "Is it possible eternally to reject injustice without ceasing
to acclaim the nature of man and the beauty of the world? Our answer is yes" (276).
[29] It may be that phrases such as this suggest the sometimes provisional nature of Camus's
disbelief.

writers continued to resort to Augustine's symbol to discuss religion's part in developing a just and humane social order. In the 1960s and 1970s, as the struggle with *mortalitas* seemed to coalesce and to intensify within the expanding cities of earth, there developed around "earthly city" a field of metaphoric significance comparable to that which once accrued to "Jerusalem," often applying to that city some of the qualities usually attributed to the heavenly Jerusalem.

One of those qualities is the harmonizing of human diversity. Charles Williams, mentioned earlier for his influence on Auden, wrote in *The Image of the City* that "the name of the city is Union." In the midst of World War II he contrasted Nazi tyranny with the ideals of the human city—communal labor, cooperation, courtesy, intelligence, and tolerance. The city does not judge, the city does not exclude. "The principle of that City," he says, "and the gates of it, are the nature of Christ as the Holy Ghost exhibits it." The variety of its citizens makes it possible for them to bear one another's burdens: each one is fitted to some task which another finds impossible for himself (101–7). John Courtney Murray, in his study of the relationship between American democratic principles and Christian belief, used the city as a metaphor for a pluralistic society united only in its willingness to seek civil agreement. Murray's book[30] argues that the modern state can seek unity without pluralism—a unity based on overt force or on the subtle coercions of propaganda, advertising, and mass amusements, all of which "operate under the name of 'freedom,' but unto the disintegration of human personality." (This, Murray says, is what Augustine meant by his "demonic" city.) But instead, society can insist on a "divine" unity, "the product of faith, reason, freedom, justice, law and love," fostering an intellectual diversity which tolerates the Christian, who brings to the city, from the kingdom of God, an affirmation of the value of each citizen's humanity (133f.).

Williams and Murray were using "city" as Augustine would have used *civitas*, to represent an entire society. In the 1960s, faced with specifically urban forms of disunity and inhumanity, other writers sought to discern the significance of Jerusalem for the political, social and economic misery of Manhattan, Birmingham, and Los Angeles. Gibson Winter, in his *The New Creation as Metropolis*,[31] approached urban social problems with an eschatological consciousness. Metropolis is Jerusalem, a vision of peace and unity; Babylon is the Standard Metropolitan Statistical Area, a state of civil chaos. To summon Christians back from "babylonian captivity" in their suburban gardens to labor at building Jerusalem, Winter fuses the millennial symbols of Revelation with socioeconomic idiom. "This New Creation," he writes, "is the final or eschatological reality, but its finality is disclosed

---

[30] John Courtney Murray, *We Hold These Truths: Catholic Reflections on the American Proposition* (Garden City, N.Y.: Doubleday Image Books, 1964).

[31] Gibson Winter, *The New Creation as Metropolis* (New York: The Macmillan Co., 1963).

through the power which it mediates in the historical present; its ultimacy is disclosed in its power as beginning of coherence and unity for metropolitan man" (133). For Winter, then, the eschatological imagination hallows the secular world, making it our home; and it hallows history, making it a process of discovering and realizing our ultimate fellowship with God.

Winter's book was followed by Harvey Cox's *The Secular City*.[32] Influenced by Camus's *The Rebel*, by Dietrich Bonhoeffer's reflections on the presence of God in an utterly secularized age, and by the confident urbanism of the early 1960s, Cox dismisses all traditional notions of church ministry and religious language as obsolete attempts to maintain a "sacred" worldview in the face of increasing human self-sufficiency. He urges religious persons to take a stand completely within the secular order—for in fact there is no other. The great cities are where humankind completes God's creation of the world. Cox envisions a new proclamation of the kingdom that would bring to the city both a healing ministry and a revolutionary deliverance from oppression. "God's action today, through secularization and urbanization, puts man in an unavoidable crisis. He must take responsibility in and for the city of man, or become once again a slave to dehumanizing powers" (132). Our choice is still between the divine *civitas* and the demonic; but Cox has so adapted Augustinian terminology that "the city of man" is his term for the human community as it manifests the kingdom.

John Dunne's *The City of the Gods*[33] is also an account of the secularization of society. And it is as well a return to Augustine's theme of *mortalitas*. The ancient city, Dunne says, was a solution to the problem of death, for people thought they could dwell there in the presence of the ever-living gods. But despairing of that unity, human beings have endlessly revised their society as they have rephrased the relationship between the living and the dead. Augustine's theory of two cities "left the Christian church in the West prepared to criticize. . . each fresh attempt of the earthly city to divinize itself but unprepared to offer any positive hope or plan for rebuilding the earthly city in a manner consistent with Christianity" (158). Dunne argues that from Augustine's account of the *civitas terrena* has sprung our deepening modern conviction of secular abandonment. This has led us to the brink of renouncing our desire "to satisfy the will to live," and discovering Christ's power to lay down life and take it up again. In that renunciation and discovery, "the city of man will have become in truth the city of God" (231).

Most of these writers render religious life in the earthly city not in the imagery of pilgrimage, but rather in the scriptural and patristic image of

---

[32] Harvey Cox, *The Secular City* (New York: The Macmillan Co., 1965).
[33] John Dunne, *The City of the Gods* (New York: The Macmillan Co., 1965). Camus is an important presence in most of Dunne's work, though only implicit in *The City of the Gods*. Augustine also figures in most of Dunne's books. Reading *The City of the Gods*, one comes to understand Camus's cryptic remark that the origins of existentialism are in Saint Augustine (*Essais*, p. 1699).

building. Traditionally the church was "edified" as it assembled evangelized men and women into a community devoted to the praise and service of God. Today "building" is often applied to Christian service in the organizations of general community welfare—organizations which, like the buildings of the secular city, are designed not for permanence but as pragmatic adaptations to short-term needs and goals, to be abandoned and eventually demolished by the discovery of new problems or new solutions.

The figure of building, however, led Jacques Ellul to a renewal of Augustinian skepticism about the secular city. In *The Meaning of the City*[34] Ellul observes that Cain's response to his expulsion from Eden was to build a city, to beget a child, and to name the city for the child. Cut off from God and alienated from nature, he inaugurated a countercreation in the human image (5f.). As a macrocosm of flawed humanity, however, the city simply magnifies those flaws and becomes the emblem of pride, cruelty, and despair. But the summons of Christ is not a call to leave the cities. The faithful, remaining there, bear the word of God into the midst of unbelievers; they "help to bring truth and reality together, to introduce somewhere, in some small way, the victory won in truth by Christ into concrete existence" (170). Yet they do not "build up" the earthly city. Ellul, spurning what he calls the "Thomist heresy," argues that human effort, whatever its spiritual motives, can in no way advance the kingdom of God in the city. The Christian takes his share in the city's work in a spirit of "active pessimism," knowing that it is only Christ's pardon, and not the convergence of human effort, that will in the end transfigure the human city. Ellul's homiletic book ends in visionary praise of the human city transformed by the grace of God, "no longer the city of war, no longer the city of slavery, no longer the world of confusion" (192).

In the work of these recent writers then, Augustine's image of the Christian situation, as that of exile in an earthly city, undergoes a certain secularization. It seeks to endow with ethical and epistemological substance the struggle of human beings with their fallibility, their hunger, their suffering, and their mortality. It is an extension of the counsel which Jeremiah offered to the exiles in Babylon:

> Yahweh Sabaoth, the God of Israel, says this to all the exiles deported from Jerusalem to Babylon, "Build houses, settle down; plant gardens and eat what they produce; take wives and have sons and daughters. . . . You must increase there and not decrease. Work for the good of the city[35] to which I have exiled you; pray to Yahweh on its behalf, since on its welfare yours depends. (Jer. 29.4–7)

Here Babylon is not a symbol of pride and harlotry, but of ordinary life. The ultimate destiny of humankind (however differently Auden and Camus con-

---

[34] Jacques Ellul, *The Meaning of the City*, trans. Dennis Pardee (Grand Rapids: William B. Eerdmans Publ. Co., 1970).
[35] "City" in Hebrew; "country" in the Septuagint.

ceived it!) is not displaced to a transhistorical city, but sought within the earthly city. And it is conceived there not in terms of power, but in images of power disavowed: common work, a vulnerable and divided city, a crucified Christ. All who dwell in the earthly city, said Augustine, are joined in the franchise of our mortality.

9

The City as Cultural Hieroglyph

BURTON PIKE
CUNY Graduate School

"C'était une ville de rêve. . ."
Il ne s'agit donc pas d'*architecture*.
—Paul Valéry

The city as an image is a peculiar trope which differs in important ways from most other images. One of its peculiarities is that it is a strongly visual figure: its basic referent is that collection of physical objects anchored in empirical space and time called the city, a place which has always been the magnet and magic center of culture, whether religious, secular, economic, artistic, or totemic. Another peculiarity is that "city" is an image with strong associations in life as well as in literature and art.

The city has been a highly charged concept through a long history of associations in Western culture, so that any literary use of it cannot help but unlock in the reader powerful affects of which he may not be entirely aware. Sociologists have shown that the ordinary city dweller, in seeking to represent his experience of city life, resorts to conventional rhetorical formulas of expression rather than attempting to individualize his own experience.[1] This suggests that a city dweller's attempts to talk about his own urban experience parallels, if on a lower plane of expression, the writer's attempt to harness the city as an image in fiction. Both writer and citizen are using the social conventions of language to express the concept of "city."

As a strongly visual image, then, and one with strong extraliterary resonances, the city as a trope cannot be regarded exclusively as a literary or linguistic figure. It is one of those symbols which, as Gilbert Durand points out, since they are not merely linguistic, exist in more than one dimension.[2] Literature involving the image of the city is thus a prime instance of art as "an original manifestation of a psycho-social function," as Durand puts it (21).

[1] See R. Richard Wohl, and Anselm L. Strauss, "Symbolic Representation and the Urban Milieu," *American Journal of Sociology*, 63, No. 5 (1958): 523–32.

[2] Gilbert Durand, *Les structures anthropologiques de l'imaginaire: Introduction à l'archétypologie générale* (N.p.: Bordas, 1969), p. 28.

Throughout the history of our culture, at least up to the early through mid-twentieth century, the city has functioned as an archetype, a continuing pattern of transmitted conventions and responses. As the word implies, an archetype is a basic model, usually a physical object like the garden, the city, or the sea, which is made the basis of a myth seen as either constantly present in history or periodically recurrent. Northrop Frye has described archetypes as "associative clusters" which "differ from signs in being complex variables. Within the complex is often a large number of specific learned associations which are communicable because a large number of people in a given culture happen to be familiar with them."[3] The physical nature of the object associated with the archetype is important: "archetypal metaphor," as Frye puts it, "involves the use of what has been called the concrete universal, the individual identified with its class, Wordsworth's 'tree of many one'" (124).

The question arises as to how the powerful "city" archetype has been transmitted through Western culture, from the Bible to Balzac to T. S. Eliot, and what it is, precisely, that has been transmitted. There are two kinds of explanation for the transmission of cultural attitudes, of which attitudes toward the city may serve as an important example. These are the "inner" and the "outer" explanations. The former follows the route initiated by Freud[4] and developed by Jung, suggesting the existence of a racial memory and a collective unconscious to explain the persistence of cultural attitudes over time. The outer explanation, on the other hand, sees sufficient basis in the historical process for this transmission, arguing that the handing down of archetypes, myths, and associations from generation to generation can be adequately accounted for by successive imprinting through oral and written means.

The inner explanation exerts a powerful attraction on the human imagination. The idea that the mind of the individual contains in some way the memory of the race is hard to resist. As Jean Starobinski notes, before going on to attack this paradigm, "the image of the past preserved *internally* is alluring, so much so that it still holds us in thrall."[5] It is alluring, Starobinski goes on to say, because it is reassuring to the individual, implying as it does that "self-knowledge is anamnesis or rememoration, and . . . that anamnesis is the recognition of deep layers (often compared to geological strata) of the present-day person" (334).

Several objections can be raised to this process as it applies to the transmission of culture. Such an internal coding would have to be genetic,

---

[3] Northrup Frye, *Anatomy of Criticism* (Princeton: Princeton University Press, 1957), p. 102.

[4] See the theory of "primal scenes" in "From the History of an Infantile Neurosis" (the Wolf Man).

[5] Jean Starobinski, "The Inside and the Outside," *Hudson Review*, 28 (1975): 333–51.

and to accept the idea that culture can be transmitted biologically one would have to accept the hypothesis that learned behavior can be genetically encoded. "Culture" is, however, a metaphysical abstraction, an amorphous concept made up of innumerable (and highly variable) bits of learned behavior which varies from one place to another and also at different times in the same place. One could argue more strongly that the basic building blocks of culture, such as reverence for and hostility toward authority, and the instinctive drive toward socialization, are biologically determined; but these cannot by themselves explain the complicated phenomenon of culture.

A more satisfactory explanation would hold that any argument for the internal preservation of the past within the individual has to be metaphorical.[6] Starobinski argues that we should look at the process of cultural transmission from the outside rather than from the inside, that we should see the distant past as consisting "in things other men have accomplished within a conceptual framework which is not and never will be ours, using a language in which we recognize nothing of ourselves. . . . The archaic world belongs to an elapsed moment; it is for us to gauge the distance separating us from it, the extent of our divergence from it, the difference on which our curiosity thrives" (334f.).

Even if one rejects the genetic explanation for the survival through time of culture attitudes, something persists which must be accounted for. Another critic, following Starobinski's line of investigation, asks: "*What is it then that persists?* What is an archetype? At best, surely, a felt presence, a sort of quark in the structure of time whose existence we can only posit as being necessary to explain the phenomenon of unintentional recurrence."[7] In other words, the concept of "archetype" satisfies the mind's basic need to see patterns everywhere in a world which remains in its essence as inscrutable to us as it must have seemed to Adam and Eve set outside the Garden of Eden.

Since "archetype" is a term which posits historical progression, we might investigate how the archetype of the city managed to become so firmly anchored in Western culture. If the genetic explanation is not sufficient, what are the historical factors which account for its persistence?

Feelings of anxiety, awe, and ambivalence toward human and divine authority were associated with the city from an early date. This association can be shown to have periodically activated, through different cultural codes, these emotions with which the city has always been linked. Joseph Rykwert has shown how, even as late as the founding of Rome, the establishment of early cities was principally a matter of ritual, designed both to propitiate the gods and to consecrate the city, whose center was regarded as the symbolic

[6] For a vatic, Jung-based argument for the internal transmission of archetypes, see Elemire Zolla, *Archetypes: The Persistence of Unifying Patterns* (New York: Harcourt, Brace, Jovanovich, 1981).

[7] Bert O. States, "The Persistence of the Archetype," *Critical Inquiry*, 7 (1980): 333–44.

intersection of the coordinate axes of the universe.[8] The growth of this ritual into myth would entail a displacement: the religious awe connected with the ceremony of the rite was internalized in the participants, where it became awe and anxiety connected with the city as the subject of the rite. This transference of affect moves from the social-ceremonial level of acting out, the level of rite, to the internalized level of myth.

The sequence from rite to myth is important: one critic has written, following Cassirer, that "in all mythical action the subject of the rite is transformed into a god or demon whom he represents. Hence . . . rites precede myth, and . . . the narrative of myth is a mediate interpretation of the immediately given rite. This explains why rites are taken so seriously in primitive religion. . . . Nature is thought to yield nothing without ceremonies."[9]

Ritualism and myth were taken up in the Bible as the basis for the figural image of the city. Equally important in the Bible is the empirical image of the city, a place in which both the confusion of daily life and the sacred moments of religious observance took place.

The Old and New Testaments are both deeply urban. Once Jerusalem became the capital of the Jewish kingdom God became its protector, so that, as James Dougherty points out, "the nomadic Yahweh accepts a permanent 'house' like the king's house and adjacent to it in the citadel on Zion."[10] In the psalms, "Temple, Zion, and Jerusalem are a nested, isomorphic 'center of the world' where the sky god makes his earthly home" (5f.). Christianity, Professor Dougherty notes, had been "a religion of city dwellers since the time of the first evangelists, organized in metropolitan districts [and] cosmopolitan in membership." Christianity "offered the urbanized Mediterranean world not a pastoral paradise, the woods and fields of Virgil's Arcadia, but a counter-city" (39).

The Bible resonates with ambivalent attitudes toward the real and the figural city; and as Christianity developed, these attitudes became incorporated in a curious kind of bifocal vision. For while the Bible posits hostility and attraction toward real cities—Rome and Jerusalem, for instance—it also presents the contrast between the real and the figural city: the earthly and heavenly Jerusalem. This bifocal vision, and the ambivalence associated with it, might have deeper roots going back to the founding of the first cities. At any rate, the biblical ambivalence toward cities, later blended with Greek

---

[8] Joseph Rykwert, *The Idea of a Town: The Anthropology of Urban Form in Rome, Italy, and the Ancient World* (Princeton: Princeton University Press, 1976), chapters 1 and 2.

[9] David Bidney, "Myth, Symbolism, and Truth," in John B. Vickery, ed., *Myth and Literature: Contemporary Theory and Practice* (Lincoln: University of Nebraska Press, 1966), p. 7.

[10] James Dougherty, *The Fivesquare City: The City in the Religious Imagination* (Notre Dame: University of Notre Dame Press, 1980), p. 5f.

and Roman elements such as the pastoral tradition, became historically imprinted on our culture in a kind of grand parabolic arc reaching from the Old and New Testaments, the Acts, Epistles, and Saint Augustine, as far as the early twentieth century.

Augustine firmly established the *topos* of this ambivalent dualism toward the city. Professor Dougherty, developing Auerbach's argument on the conflict between reality and figural representation, notes that "with Augustine's two cities"—Rome and Jerusalem—"the relationship between 'figure' and 'reality' fluctuates treacherously" (30). Augustine, well aware of the complexities of real cities, nevertheless wanted to press them symbolically into dramatized allegorical images. For this purpose they had to be simplified. Thus Rome, in the dramatized figural scheme, was reduced to the symbol of worldly sinfulness, while Jerusalem became entirely the emblem of eschatological vision. "Augustine's figural view of history does not permit him to look closely or comprehensively at the physical reality which carries significance. In allegory, the physical characteristics of the image are reduced to only those appropriate to the controlling idea" (31). And "since Rome attains significance only by figural identification with Babylon, and thus by its opposition to Jerusalem, Augustine can only posit a relationship of hostility between the two cities. God has written history in antitheses" (35).

During the Dark Ages, cities as centers of culture largely disappeared in Europe and, as Lewis Mumford argues, had to be essentially reinvented in the Middle Ages. In the interim, the essential cultural structures survived in the monasteries, religious institutions organized along urban lines.[11] When cities revived in Europe, the monasteries contributed their physical and social patterns, as well as their store of knowledge, to the cities. The amalgamated biblical, classical, and Augustinian archetype of the city was reestablished along with the cities themselves.

The case for the historical transmission of cultural attitudes toward the city in Western culture seems persuasive. It can be refined by the addition of E. H. Gombrich's concept of the schema or adapted stereotype, which provides a more detailed framework for explaining how conventions in painting and literature function in the process of historical transmission. Gombrich's thesis is that an artist does not begin a painting by observing reality, but from a preexisting model in his mind to which he makes the empirical object conform. This mental model, or schema, is derived from the conventions and prevailing modes of art at the time. The schema is, in effect, the set of reigning conventions which unites the vision of the artist with the audience's ability to recognize that vision. Thus a painter depicts a landscape by making it conform to a preexisting set of conventions understood by both

---

[11] Lewis Mumford, *The City in History: Its Origins, its Transformations, and its Prospects* (New York: Harcourt, Brace and World, 1961), pp. 246–48.

the painter and his viewers[12]—an argument which can easily be extended to the language of literature.

Gombrich's schemata are, of course, historical conventions and as such subject to change over time; but they do not ordinarily change very rapidly, especially where a broad public is concerned, or a conservative royal court. This slowness of change provides for the continuity of archetypal associations, which contain, to repeat Frye, "a large number of specific learned associations which are communicable because a large number of people in a given culture happen to be familiar with them."

If conventions change abruptly, there is a "drag time" until the general public catches up, reestablishing communication between artist and audience on the basis of a new set of conventions. When, however, the culture itself goes through a rapid series of radical dislocations, such as has happened in the last hundred years, the pattern for transmission of traditional archetypes may be broken, and the new set of conventions may be discontinuous with the old.

To illustrate archetypal attitudes toward the city in a text from the late history of this archetype, I would like to examine an 1856 entry from the *Journals* of Edmond and Jules de Goncourt. Following that, by way of contrast, I would like to substantiate what seems to me the disappearance of this archetypal *topos* in our own time, as illustrated by a present-day American text.

The entry from the Goncourt *Journals* is a nonfictional text written by quondam novelists. It is halfway between an objective description of a scene actually observed and a literary representation of the scene:

> Back from a day in the country, we dined this evening at La Terrasse, a sleazy restaurant covered with badly gilded trellises around which climb a dozen shriveled vines, and we have across the way from us the setting sun lighting up with its last rays the shrill colors of the posters one can see above the Panorama Arcade. Never, it seems to me, were my eye and heart more rejoiced than by the sight of this ugly thick plaster assaulted by huge letters and scrawled over, dirtied, and smeared with the advertisements of Paris. Here everything is by man and belongs to man, with the bare exception of a sickly tree growing out of a crack in the asphalt, and these leprous house-fronts speak to me as nature never has. The generations of our time are too civilized, too old, too deeply enamored of the factitious and the artificial to be amused by the green of the earth and the blue of the sky. And here I shall make a strange confession: in front of the canvas of a good landscape painter I feel myself more in the country than when I am in the middle of a field or the woods.[13]

---

[12] E. H. Gombrich, *Art and Illusion: A Study in the Psychology of Pictorial Representation*, Bollingen Series 85 (Princeton: Princeton University Press, 1972 [1961]), pp. 87–90.

[13] Edmond and Jules de Goncourt, *Journal: Mémoires de la vie littéraire*, édition definitive (Paris: Flammarion, n.d.), 1:105f. Entry for 1 July 1856; translation mine.

The schema to which this observed scene is made to correspond is the conventional opposition between country and city, a remnant of the pastoral tradition. The Goncourts achieve their effect by reversing the values traditionally associated with this *topos*. Instead of presenting the country as a healing escape from the bustle of the city, as the pastoral tradition would have it, they find relief in escaping from the country back to the city. This means that the Goncourts are still able to activate the pastoral code in their readers, and to create surprise and perhaps shock by reversing its traditional associations.

The authors add bite to this reversal by praising the city in its most tawdry aspect: their collective "eye and heart" are "rejoiced" by badly gilded trellises and the smeared advertisements of the city. Their organs of perception and emotion are also gladdened by two scrawny survivals of the natural world in this sleazy cityscape, "a dozen shriveled vines" and "a sickly tree growing out of a crack in the asphalt." The healthy vegetation of the countryside they have just returned from is not described. Nature can be appreciated in a painting (in specifying "the canvas of a *good* landscape painter," the *"badly* gilded trellises," and other features of this scene, the Goncourts flaunt their aesthetic perception of reality) but not as itself, because—and this is the heart of their observation—"the generations of our time are too civilized, too old, too deeply enamored of the factitious and the artificial to be amused by the green of the earth and the blue of the sky." While the shabby objects of this urban scene have been lovingly described, the countervailing natural world is reduced to the two colors, blue and green. There is no counterpresentation of what the countryside looked like on their outing, where they were, what they saw. The country is absent from the text.

Thus the Goncourts use the city as a crystallizing image for a cultural generalization ("the generations of our time"). They concretize the abstract categories of the factitious and artificial by the sleazy restaurant, the ugly plaster, and the smeared posters. The Paris of monuments, the city of power and beauty, the capital of the nineteenth century, is nowhere to be seen. This is not an impression of a heavenly city but of a ruthlessly terrestrial one. And the shriveled vines and sickly tree are presented as urban artifacts rather than reminders of a rural idyll; they are blasted life forms from some unimaginable other world.

The Goncourts are not simply expressing their personal reactions but claiming to make a general cultural statement they know their readers will understand. They are articulating for their readers a received attitude, the debilitated aestheticism of a bourgeois society which has lost its capacity for strong feeling, a society which looks for pleasure to a grimy urban setting rather than to the image of a magnificent (read "heavenly") city or the pristine world of nature.

For reasons which are not readily apparent and which deserve further

investigation,[14] the negative values associated with the image of the city
grew steadily stronger in the nineteenth century from Balzac onwards.
While the city remained the magnet and magic center of cultural life, and
while material conditions of life in cities were improving at the most rapid
rate in history, attitudes toward the city emphasized increasingly what I
would call the city's negative acoustics. An early stage of this process, along
with the fragmentation of the image of the city, may be discerned in the
passage from the Goncourts.

Through the early years of the twentieth century, the negative and
fragmented treatment of the city in art grew into a reigning convention.
Anxiety, isolation, and apathy were the characteristics of city life singled out
most frequently by writers. The artistic devices used to present the city took
the form of fragmentation of the observed urban scene and fragmentation of
the urban personality. To name examples from literature is to list most of the
important writers of the time: Eliot, Joyce, Pound, Rilke, Kafka, Musil,
Proust, Brecht.

The fragmentation of the city's image of course reflects the larger
perception of the fragmentation of Western society in general, which has
been increasing over the last hundred years. The social community of
accepted and shared common values has in this time definitively come loose
from its moorings and drifted out to sea. Thus Nietzsche told us that God is
dead and we have killed him; thus Rilke exclaims in one of the *Sonnets to
Orpheus* (2.26): "Alas, where are we? Freer and freer/ like kites torn loose we
chase in midair, with windily tattered/ edges of laughter." Harvey Cox
expresses this loss of moorings another way when he speaks of "an elemental
principle now determining twentieth-century society—that our *functional*
relationships to each other in communities of common interest have become
more important than our *geographic* communities. This is in fact the basic
motif of what we designate urbanization."[15]

A new element has recently been added to this ubiquitous sense of
fragmentation in life and art: the prospect that for the first time the extinction
of the human race is easily within our power. This places the whole of our
cultural history in question, definitively separating the present from the
past. Until very recently the destruction of the world had always been a
metaphor. As we look to the future, T. S. Eliot's "Tradition and the Individual Talent," with its assumption of slow accretion and incremental change, is
impossible to imagine. The prophetic and valedictory quality of Yeats's line,

[14] See Robert Nisbet, *Sociology as an Art Form* (London: Oxford University Press, 1976),
esp. chapter 6, "The Rust of Progress," and Burton Pike, *The Image of the City in Modern
Literature* (Princeton: Princeton University Press, 1981), *passim*.
[15] Harvey Cox, *The Secular City: Secularization and Urbanization in Theological Perspective*, rev. ed. (New York: Macmillan, 1968), p. 194. See also Alvin B. Kernan, *The
Imaginary Library: An Essay on Literature and Society* (Princeton: Princeton University
Press, 1982).

"ancient lineaments are blotted out," seems closer to where we stand now, on the edge of an eschatological vision of a kind never dreamt in *Revelation*.

The image of the city in contemporary literature reflects this changed view. Literary cities have become as disembodied and fragile as have character, action, and form. The city continues to loom large for us because it remains, if no longer a biblical-classical archetype, still the matrix of culture. Donald Barthelme's remarkable story "City Life" presents, in a droll but at the same time frightening way, the fragmented, secular anomie which characterizes contemporary urban life. Barthelme pushes the visions of urban fragmentation found in Kafka and Eliot into a surrealism which is, in its effect, extremely realistic. In Barthelme's story the past is a fugitive memory in the mind of the reader, not a component of the characters, and an earlier generation's "age of anxiety" has given way to an age of anomie. As one of the characters in "City Life" puts it, "the problem today is not angst but lack of angst."[16]

In this story two girls move to the city—New York, the capital of the twentieth century—and enter law school. Elsa, the extrovert, has a boy-friend, Charles, but marries another man, Jacques, without much thought in either direction. Ramona, the introvert, lives a rich inner life: she spends most of her time brooding about the city. In the course of the series of fragmentary vignettes of which the story consists, Ramona gives birth to a child. It is, she maintains, a virgin birth. She is not able to ascribe paternity to the singer Moonbelly, to Charles, or to Vercingetorix, leader of the firemen. "The engendering force was, perhaps, the fused glance of all of them," Ramona muses. "From the millions of units crawling about on the surface of the city, their wavering desirous eyes selected me. The pupil enlarged to admit more light: more me" (167f). The baby is named Sam. The shards of the big-city world to which Ramona proclaims Sam's virgin birth greet her claim with skepticism and indifference. City lives proceed as before, unreconciled among the stars.

This story bristles with an arsenal of devices for communication: television, telephone, letters, conversations, songs, sex, eyes, even mental telepathy. The characters, however, live in states of partial or total anomie: what happens happens, and nothing seems to matter. Each act in the story, such as the bizarre kidnapping of Charles from Cleveland, is both reported and received with the matter-of-fact indifference which is so characteristic of our compartmentalized urban culture. Even the virgin birth of Sam, which none of the characters in the story connect with any other virgin birth, is not the stuff of which a religion, a myth, or a legend can be made. It is just another accidental happening, like the blackout in New York of which Ramona thinks. History is present to the characters only in the form of old Wendell Corey movies they watch on television. Barthelme's prose is of a piece with

---

[16] Donald Barthelme, *City Life* (New York: Farrar, Straus, and Giroux, 1970), p. 165.

the world it presents: one critic has called his writing "a transistorized or 'software' discourse."[17]

The city is the great presence in this story; the human figures are only functions, puppets even, of the inscrutable and vaguely menacing emitter of mysterious forces which is the city. This city consists of lines of force rather than described places. As Ramona implies, the city itself may be the begetter of her child. Modern life is urban life; the *urbs* has totally swallowed up both the *civitas* and the *orbis*. And this *urbs* is more like a lunar landscape than a human community. There is no way to think of it as either an earthly or a heavenly Jerusalem.

Culture, in the sense of a connective tissue linking the present to the past, has become a joke Barthelme plays on the reader, far beyond the dazed understanding of his drifting characters. It is as if Barthelme posits the reader as belonging to the last generation of those who would have any associations whatever with the past. "Vercingetorix" is the name capriciously bestowed on the fire chief, while the reader struggles in vain to establish a connection with the dim historical figure in his memory which does not exist in the text. The reader also struggles with the virgin birth of Sam, trying to relate it to the Christian tradition, but this is an equally futile exercise. These sounds from the past echo in the reader, not in the story; the author invokes them to demonstrate the discontinuity between the associations of the past and the urban culture of the present. In short, the city in "City Life" does not function as an archetype: it does not activate responses in the reader which have been prepared, through education and convention, for assimilating the image of the city, as the Goncourts' audience was prepared to assimilate even a reversal of the pastoral convention.

I suggested earlier that the archetype of the city as it existed for two thousand years has come to an end as the result of major discontinuities in our world and its values. It follows that to continue to speak of the city as an archetype in contemporary literature would be to apply a term which does not fit the circumstances. It is in this context that I would like to suggest the term "cultural hieroglyph" as best representing the way the city image now functions in literature.[18]

"Hieroglyphic" refers to the ancient Egyptian system of writing in which figures or objects are used to represent words or sounds. More

---

[17] Perry Meisel, "Mapping Barthelme's 'Paraguay'," in *Fragments: Incompletion and Discontinuity, New York Literary Forum* 8–9, general editor Jeanine Parisier Plottel, guest editor Lawrence D. Kritzman (New York: New York Literary Forum, 1981): 131.

[18] I derived the term from François le Lionnais's "psychological hieroglyphics" by way of Howard Nemerov, "On Poetry and Painting, with a Thought of Music," in W. J. T. Mitchell, ed., *The Language of Images* (Chicago: University of Chicago Press, 1980), p. 13. For a historical overview of the concept and term "hieroglyphic," see Liselotte Dieckmann, *Hieroglyphics: The History of a Literary Symbol* (Saint Louis: Washington University Press, 1970).

generally, a hieroglyph is a picture or symbol with a hidden meaning, an emblem: this use of the term derives from neoplatonic and occult traditions. Hieroglyphic also means, by extension, "hard to read; illegible; undecipherable."[19] It is above all a *visual* image, exemplifying Wittgenstein's maxim that "a *picture* held us captive. And we could not get outside it, for it lay in our language and language seemed to repeat it to us inexorably."[20]

The advantage of using the term "cultural hieroglyph" rather than "archetype" in discussing contemporary literature of the city follows both from its visual orientation and from the fragmented and ahistorical nature of most serious mid-twentieth-century urban literature. Whereas "archetype" is by definition a term of historical process, "hieroglyph" refers directly to discrete objects or signs in themselves. In the passage from the Goncourt *Journals* quoted above, the city was still operating, for both the authors and their readers, as an archetype linked to a long chain of historically transmitted associations, even though the values were reversed. In Barthelme's "City Life," however, the city functions as a cultural hieroglyph. If Barthelme's city has a hidden meaning or is an emblem of something, it is inscrutable, illegible, and undecipherable.

Of course, for literature to function at all as a medium of communication there must be a common understanding between writer and audience.[21] Barthelme's hieroglyphic city can be seen as employing a contemporary convention for which the reader has been prepared by three-quarters of a century of literary change, as well as by the serious dislocations in modern life generally. Barthelme's verbal city is, after all, a city the reader recognizes. So the process continues, by which the writer operates with conventions to which the reader responds. That process must continue if literature is to be read; but different terms are called for. The archetype of the city still performs a valuable function when applied to its long but finite trajectory from the Bible and the classical world to the literature of the early twentieth century; but it has lost its hold on the present.

[19] *American Heritage Dictionary.*

[20] "Ein *Bild* hielt uns gefangen. Und heraus konnten wir nicht, denn es lag in unserer Sprache, und sie schien es uns nur unerbittlich zu wiederholen." *Philosophical Investigations,* 2nd bilingual edition, trans. G. E. M. Anscombe (New York: Macmillan, 1958), p. 48 (par. 115).

[21] On this point see Frank Kermode, *The Sense of an Ending* (London: Oxford University Press, 1967), p. 102.